STREETPLONK 2000

'With his corking reviews and flair for quips,
His nose has launched a thousand sips'

(Ann Smallman's winning entry in the
Superplonk 99 competition)

'Mr Gluck makes a charming and witty host'

Guardian

'A truly unpretentious wine writer is a rare beast, and Gluck
is not just unpretentious but clear, straightforward and –
sometimes brutally – frank'

Hampstead & Highgate Express

'For a clear and unpretentious guide to what is eminently
drinkable on the supermarket shelf, there is none better
than Malcolm Gluck's *Superplonk*'

Edinburgh Evening News

'For those intent on drinking their way through the fes-
tivities, Malcolm Gluck's *Superplonk* and *Streetplonk* are
invaluable stocking fillers'

Solicitors Journal

Streetplonk 2000

Malcolm Gluck

CORONET BOOKS

Hodder & Stoughton

First published in Great Britain as
a Coronet paperback original in 1999.

10 9 8 7 6 5 4 3 2 1

A CIP Catalogue record for this title is available
from the British Library

ISBN 0 340 71314 3

Typeset by Palimpsest Book Production Limited,
Polmont, Stirlingshire
Printed and bound in Great Britain by
Mackays of Chatham PLC, Chatham, Kent

Hodder and Stoughton
A division of Hodder Headline
338 Euston Road
London NW1 3BH

To Diane Rowley – who helps so much

'Go where you are going, warily. And report back.'

Edwin Brock

Streetplonk 2000

CONTENTS

INTRODUCTION

I must come clean. I can deceive you no longer. I owe it to the arrival of the new millennium to put the record straight.

I am an almost complete fraud. I am not the writer many people take me for. The truth is this: more often than not I expend no more effort on bag-packing before I write about the wines of far-flung vineyards than that required to load my cycle pannier with a notepad and pencil (and the A-to-Z).

Yet many people, even some readers, insist on regarding me as a globe-trotter. They never cease to view me as an exotic, peripatetic creature whose healthy tan owes everything to following the sun. Where have you just come back from? they ask. Battersea, I mutter. Or it might be Woking (if I'm really in luck). My tan, I explain, is nothing more than a healthy glow brought out by saddle-borne excess. I travel by intercontinental airliner less than any other decently-published wine writer I know (the poorly-published wine hack, with leisure time to burn, seems to spend, at someone else's expense, four fifths of her un-inky-fingered life lounging beside sun-drenched *vitis vinifera* plants). But I? But I, though shaped for sportive tricks and cheered to court an amorous airways drinking glass, must needs pass up the drunken reveries of the idling vineside dozer, for I am required to make my merry meetings in Britain – my steaming deskbound word processor, in many instances, only pedalling distance away. Why? Because I must before all else put my readers; must consider my wine guides; must look above all other things to the wines which line the shelves of the supermarkets and high street wine chains. My priorities are clear. I need to taste the wines the reader will find in the shops and this means regularly visiting the offices of these establishments to taste their wines.

I can, however, travel in my mind. In 1998, I visited a score of wine countries in this fashion. Amongst other armchair travels, I delved into the motivations of the international flying winemaker (but never toured further than Oxford), I was intimate with Austria (and merely cycled to Knightsbridge), I was entertained by Western Australia (handily situated just off Regent Street), I stopped off in Bulgaria (and never put a foot further east than an eastern orthodox chapel in a mews behind the Albert Hall); I meditated on claret (and went no nearer Bordeaux than Blackfriars Bridge) and I toured Spain (making my notes in a tapas bar in Portobello Road, London, W11). Oh yes ... I also studied the new dynamics emerging within the northern Italian wine industry. And here I did have to pocket my passport. The indulgent reader, however, will surely feel that this last excursion served purely the interests of insight (which anyone who has ever eaten supper – risotto and rabbit in my case – beside Orvieto's delicious floodlit cathedral will readily concede is a forgivable lapse into authenticity).

Let me begin, though, with Oxford – city of aspiring dreams – where I came to eat at the Cherwell Boathouse Restaurant, to lunch with an international jet-setting wine maker, Gaetane Carron, who had given up the chance to doss down in a chateau in France and/or eat oysters in a Pacific-front apartment in Chile to base herself in this snotty spot.

Why should any wine maker give Oxford a second thought? It is a cruelly selfish city, famed for motor manufacture, notorious for possessing a brazen council estate, and infamed for turning out *soi-disant* egg-heads many of which are addled. There is nothing in the way of vineyards, the odd back garden fruit trellis hardly counts, and it is far off the world's vinous trade routes. Oxford's contribution to wine is two-fold: the donnish consumption of it – cobwebby stuff served up at college table feasts by liveried serfs – and the tertiary educating of wine celebrities Oz Clarke, Charles Mecalfe, Andrew Barr, Jancis

Robinson, Anthony Rose, Giles MacDonagh, and doubtless several others.

Nevertheless, to Oxford I came, note-booketed, tape-recorder-ready, sniffing at a glass of 1991 Clos de la Barre, staring at Oxford's newest resident wine maker over the lunch table. Why would a disgracefully young, cultured, intelligent, personable woman of the world, speaking many languages, who has worked in wine in Beaune, the Medoc, Pommard, Alsace, Italy, New South Wales, Oregon, California, and, latterly, Chile, where she was part of the team which makes one of my favourite red and white pairs (Concha y Toro Casillero del Diablo Sauvignon Blanc and Cabernet Sauvignon, both ridiculously good value under a fiver apiece), decide to come and make her base and her bed within the noxiously fumacious environs of Oxford?

Let me, first, give you the answers she gave me (between glasses of the Clos de la Barre which we drank with a salad of black pudding and a red pepper and aubergine gratin). Ms Carron smiles with her eyes. You believe every word she says.

'I'm on a mission here,' she told me. 'The more good quality wines we can get on the market the better for all of us. I'm all for making the best wine we can at the lowest possible price because we need to get more and more people drinking wine.'

More people drinking wine? Goodness – the woman's a saint. Hmm. But why Oxford? What has Oxford got which isn't to be found anywhere else?

'There's no particular reason really. It could have been anywhere, it could have been Scotland. It had to be Britain because the company I'm making wine for, Western Wines of Shropshire, is based in Britain.'

I should explain here that Western Wines is one of the more dynamic and resourceful (and, for drinkers, the least well-known since it works behind closed trade-only doors) creations of the UK wine boom. Our thirst for highly fruity but lowly priced wines has seen the setting up of several groups specialising in employing wine makers like Gaetane solely to make wine for their customers. These customers include many of our noblest wine retailers who ask Western Wines either to make wines to order or come to the company to see what is currently being made, or is under development, which they can buy 'ready-made' and sell to the likes of you and me. This is a company adventurous enough to launch a 3-litre wine box called Two Tribes, consisting of a blend of Chilean and Argentinian wine. Gaetane is directly responsible for overseeing production of some 600,000 cases of wine and she has ten wine makers answering to her in Spain, France, Italy, Greece and South Africa. (Who knows if she won't make an attempt to master Greek and Afrikaans during all those air flights she'll have to make? The other languages trip fluently off her tongue already.)

Was Oxford, then, just going to be a glorified dosshouse for this globe-trotting *française*? I put it to her, refilling her glass, straight: 'So there wasn't something about Oxford? Something you came here and discovered and fell in love with?'

'Well,' she said, 'I'd never seen England before. London, yes – during the summer of '89 when I worked in a wine shop after leaving the University of Paris. That's all I knew of England.' She looks wistful; inhales the glorious feral aroma from her glass of the Clos de la Barre.

'I like England a lot – I don't know why. I didn't know Oxford. I didn't know it was such a big city . . . all those traffic jams . . .'

Very attractive personality, Gaetane Carron. She's very fit, very polished, tremendously self-sustained – and behind all that seeming openness and unflinching eye-contact and lovely smile . . . exceedingly elusive.

Well, Ms Carron is a Frenchwoman. We all know about Frenchwomen don't we? We've all read *Les Liaisons Dangereuses* (twice in my case and a third reserved for the next long holiday). We've all seen *Un homme et une femme*. Gaetane Carron can't pull the wool over my mince pies.

Gaetane is a hedonist. She lives in Oxford purely to be able to walk out of her house, cross a main road, trot down a little alleyway leading to the river, and within minutes of closing her front door have her feet under a table at the Cherwell Boathouse restaurant. This is a restaurant which hates piped music, frowns on smoking before 10.30pm, and offers up unpretentious yet flavour-packed food. Stuff Oxford's more celebrated chef and eatery: Ray White and his stuffy *Manoir aux Quatres Saisons*, with its temple-like pretensions and refusal to take back faulty wines (a boring story I won't here bore you with). Here, by the Cherwell, Gaetane can drink Clos de la Barre and eat any number of interesting dishes, none of which is outrageously priced or eclectically modern or too trendy. Best of all, there is the restaurant's personality-packed wine list to peruse, to salivate over, to swim in (and admire for its reasonable prices); for the place is owned by Anthony Verdin, partner in a small London wine merchant, Morris & Verdin, specialising in wines from all over the world but distinguished by individuality and verve. This is the answer to the question as to why anyone would want to live in Oxford. Gaetane is a woman who is patently unimpressed by motor cars or dons. She prefers jogging and mountain bicycles. She couldn't give a nail clipping for any of the dreams within those spires. The fact is that Gaetane Carron is in love with Clos de la Barre, or rather, if you ask me, the man who makes it, one Dominique Lafon, and there is no better place to drink such stunning Meursault, one of the genuinely great, concentrated, utterly ravishing white wines in the world, than this charmingly woody, riparian restaurant. And if Monsieur Lafon doesn't take her fancy, she could, at the time we ate there, turn to wines from Alsace (made by Andre Ostertag), California (Paul Draper, Randall Graham – both ex-pro philosophers), plus an abundance of other fascinating wines – from New Zealand, Portugal, the Loire, Germany, Languedoc, etcetera – almost every one of which is made by a good looking, outrageously talented bloke. Do I need to go into more details?

Of course Ms Carron herself wouldn't admit to anything more than mild flirtation with this bunch of guys. But I know better. All that baloney about 'being on a mission', about 'having to be in the UK', about 'loving England' ! You see, Gaetane, you gave yourself away the moment you saw those words on the restaurant's wine list. Those wonderful, heart-and-palate-rending words: Comtes Lafon Meursault Clos de la Barre 1991. I have your whoop of joy on tape.

Now what will the alert reader learn from all this? The cynic will riposte, suffocating under his indignation, that the episode retailed above is nothing more than the indulgent blatherings of an esurient wine hack enjoying lunch with an attractive woman. But consider. What did we discover here about the nature of the flying wine maker? Did we, as many wine writers have suggested, merely find confirmation that these creatures are intent on making uniformly fruity, cheap, conveyor-belt non-entities with no regional character or typicity whatsoever? No, we did not. What impresses when one tastes these wines is certainly a clarity of fruitiness and modern wine making methods but the difference between La Luna e i Falo Barbera d'Asti 1995 and Gouts et Couleurs Syrah/Mourvedre 1997 is one which faithfully preserves the typicity of the region. The modernity has permitted the fruit to express itself in each case with greater freshness and flavour without conceding anything to some vague idea of uniformity of style. Also impressive is the number of wines which Gaetane and her team of wine makers have made and developed in so many countries. In Italy, there are 26 wines (from Frascati down to Puglia); in France, there are 45 wines (including several developed for the last world cup) and they include Cotes du Ventoux, Vin de Pays Vaucluse, Cotes-du-Rhone Villages, Gigondas, Anjou Rose, Muscadet and Macon Vinzelles; and 18 in Spain mostly involving the tempranillo grape.

I met in Oxford an extreme individualist who would wish at all costs to preserve the individuality of the wines under her supervision. Meeting a flying wine maker like Gaetane Carron confirms that such a person could not, in a million years, routinely trot out boring, recipe-made, oven-ready wines.

Now the same thing can be said, attitudinally, of the vast majority of Austrian wine makers. Yes, I did say Austria. Sorry.

Did I just spot a stifled yawn? Quite understandable. Austria isn't Australia is it? Even if you say it slowly.

Yet Austria is by far the most eccentric wine nation in Europe. Alas, its whacky populace doesn't immediately evoke sunshine and joyful carousing amongst the vines. If it summons up anything at all, it is of course anti-freeze.

Do you need reminding of the notorious Austrian wine fraud of 1985? A handful of barmy Austrian wine merchants added diethylene glycol to grape juice so that they could pass off the ripeness level of the grapes as higher than it was in reality and so charge a greater price for the eventual wine. You may ask how they were rumbled. Can you believe the barmiest of these crooks claimed the outlay on glycol as a legitimate business expense in order to reduce his taxable income? The tax inspector noticed this and thought to himself . . . funny. It beggars belief . . . no, of course it doesn't. These crooks were Austrians. Even the crooks in Austria are totally out to lunch.

I am pleased to have an excuse to write about this mad country. Austrian wine trickles – it cannot be said to surge – in my veins. My grandfather was an Austrian and so I am out to lunch some of the time, too. To me, restaurants are laboratories.

It is possible, more than likely in fact, that grandad drank not only Austrian wine but the stuff from Vienna itself. Vienna may summon up images of *wiener schnitzel, apfel strudel,* Mozart, the Spanish Riding School, *sachertorte* chocolate cake, Schnitzler's orgiastic theatre, the Danube, and the invention of the *croissant,* but for 600 Viennese wine growers Vienna is about growing wine. 600! To give you a point of comparison, that is two thirds of the total number of wine growers in the whole US of A. Vienna is – proof of eccentricity on an epic scale – the world's only city with such claim to metropolitan vineyard ownership (Paris, for instance, manages just one, a tiny green shrine in Montmartre).

The Austrians, then, we can take it, adore wine. Consider the facts. With a population of a mere seven million plus they manage to guzzle 250-million litres of wine a year and grow around 200-million litres. With such a crazy thirst who's worried about export? The UK sips a little: mostly well-known high street wines like Lenz Moser Gruner Veltliner or the cheekily fresh red Blauer Zweigelt.

In the past, though, one Austrian wine in particular was nigh on being a household word in this country and it was made by the same Lenz Moser company. It is a word I am not likely to forget: Schluck! My name, and I was a schoolboy when the wine was current, conveniently matched it (amongst other more obscene coincidental rhymes). It took that 1985 wine scandal to bury Schluck – not because it was contaminated but because it was Austrian. Austrian wine was a tougher proposition to sell in the UK in the middle 1980s than a pair of skis to a one-legged Bedouin.

Herr Lenz Moser, and there is such a personage, can trace the family's involvement in wine back to 1124. However, the opprobrium attaching to Austrian wine as a result of the scandal forced the company to sell itself in 1985 to a conglomerate and until recently Herr Moser continued to run the business.

I can testify to how seriously Herr Moser is out to lunch because late last year he invited me out to lunch with him, and to taste his wines, in a restaurant, excuse me *laboratory*, in Knightsbridge, a little way down from Harvey Nichols. He never breathed a word to me at that time that he was moving out (to work with Mondavi, the Californian wine company). Perhaps I should have guessed when he, representative of an established European wine dynasty, astounded me by saying 'I really think new world wine makers are the future. I'm very fond of zinfandel.' But at the time I passed this remark off as just another Austrian eccentricity – like the restaurant. This was, and is, an extravagant establishment called Vong – after its chef Jean-Georges Vongerichten. It offers a 'beautifully realised fantasy' which is 'an adventurous deviation from traditional French flavours . . . uplifted by . . . Thai herbs and spices.' Why did Herr Moser choose such an unusual kitchen for his wines?

Because he is an Austrian, born and bred. His wines put up a brave fight. The gruner veltliner, dry and rich, went with the chicken coconut soup (with galangal and shitake mushrooms); the pinot blanc was a cosy companion for the prawn satay and its oyster sauce; the Siegendorf 1995, the first red, went sort-of okay with the quail 'rubbed with Thai spices'; the cabernet franc was a mite overwhelmed by the duck breast with tamarind and sesame sauce, and the fabulously sweet, honeyed Trockenbeerenauslese 1995 was simply unforgettable with a roast Asian pear with licorice ice-cream.

Eccentric meal I hear you mutter and you would be right. I can't think of many wine producers who would be keen to pit their bottles against such unusual food. But this is *Austria* we're talking about here. Doing the sensible, boring, predictable thing doesn't come into it.

It isn't only with wine and food that Austrians are out of their trees. The year before last, I received through the post a compact disc from Herr Willi Opitz, who has his vineyards (all five acres of them) south east of Vienna, ten miles from the Hungarian border. At the time Herr Opitz worked in a pet-food factory (as an engineer, I discovered, when I eventually met him) but now he's tending his vines full time. Such serious employment does not, however, in any way lessen Herr Opitz's waggish sense of humour. Do you know how he spent his Christmas Eve four years ago? You can't imagine, so I will tell you. He recorded the sounds of his wines fermenting. Not just one wine, not just a few moments of 'plop, plip, plop' and 'plip, plop, plip' but a dozen different wines, each with its own sound track.

Now my wife is a game girl. She's married to me, for one thing. I played her the 'Sound of Wine' as the CD is sedately called and she ran screaming from the room after less than a minute. 'Why don't you give it to someone you don't like?' she yelled. Naturally, I was appalled at her cruel suggestion but it gave me an idea. I would like to give the CD to someone yes, but not someone I don't like. May I offer it to the reader of this book who writes me (c/o the publisher) the most entertaining letter? It'll give me something to publish in the introduction to the next edition of *Streetplonk*. I must warn you, though, my wife is right. The 'Sound of Wine' is the aural equivalent of the Chinese water torture.

Not so Austrian wines. They are complex and quirky and it is to be regretted that they are so expensive and only to be found at out-of-the-way emporia. This is the reason examples of them are such rarities in this book.

The same could almost be said of the wines of Western Australia.

Naturally I have a soft spot for Western Australia. It was here that I first slept with a wine maker. He was a civilised fellow; read an improving book before he dropped off; didn't snore; wasn't demanding with the use of the loo the next morning.

Of course I felt a little guilty. One does in circumstances like that and the circumstances were that unless one of us, and it was the spin of a coin which decided who, took the camp bed the motel offered and shared the only vacant room, we were, as far as accommodation was concerned that night in the one-horse hamlet of Pemberton, up a *eucalyptus myrtaceae* – that is to say a gum tree. And such forestry is very thick on the ground in WA.

Sheep are another significant feature of the landscape. They represent one vivid reason why Western Australia, isolated beyond its three deserts (the Gibson, Great Victoria and Great Sandy), is looked down upon by the snootier wine regions of the country, the upper and lower Hunter Valleys, Barossa, Coonawarra, McLaren Vale, Yarra Valley, and so on, which have over the past fifteen years acquired minor but solid international reputations for the fulsomeness of their fruit and the perceived paradisical locations of their vineyards. But Western Australia is not so regarded. If one were to propose an animal to represent the State it is not a kangaroo or a wallaby which springs to mind, it is an underdog.

I like underdogs. They are the only pets, hobby horses apart, I am prepared unconditionally to offer love (my children have cats, true, but we pass on opposite sides of the stairs). And when the underdog *becomes* a hobby horse, what a fantastic creature we then have!

Western Australia, let me tell you, is the most individualistic of Australia's six states and it stands no nonsense from anyone. Whilst modern Aussies debate the touchy subject of the country becoming a republic, it was WA which as far back as 1933 voted to secede from the Commonwealth. (I was also told, by a grizzled Sydney bar historian of doubtful sobriety, that the Australian government was prepared to offer WA as a sop to the Japanese during an invasion scare around the time of the last world war.) This individuality is fully reflected in the wines it produces. It is patently a very happy place to plant vines and it is why so many of its fruits, red, white, sweet, sparkling, are so cheerful in their turn. Why else am I trotting around the Cafe Royal, sited in the most perfectly curvaceous yet noisiest and most traffic polluted part of London's historic Regent Street, with such a contented smile on my face? It is the occasion of the 1998 Australian Wine Show, the opportunity to taste hundreds of wines from scores of wineries from every nook of the sprawling island so prosaically named – Australia deriving simply from *Australis* meaning, ho hum, southern land – and I am determined that the only wines I will examine today are from the even more prosaically named Western Southern Land. Many an exhibitor, offering me some rare red from Eden Valley or Clare, feigns affront at my refusal and then, when I explain that once astride his hobby horse the dedicated rider never swaps mounts, looks at me as if I am mad.

Even Penfolds, the giant Aussie producer, affects to be upset as I steadfastly canter past the company's main stand, pausing only to refresh myself with a couple of wines, a Cabernet Merlot 1995 and a Chardonnay 1996, from the single Penfolds vineyard holding in W. Aus, Devil's Lair. This 85-acre vineyard is so named because it is near an historic cave, a hidey-hole for indigenes for over 7000 years before the vine growers turned up, in which have been discovered fossilised remnants of *Sarcophilus ursinus*, the legendary and fearsomely sanguinary sheep-eating Tasmanian Devil which is a sort of cross between a disgruntled weasel and a sore-headed bear. The two wines I tasted from here, made by Janice McDonald, are well in this monstrous tradition being huge, flavoursome, molar-crunching specimens full of character and complexity. The little region of WA they are grown in is called Margaret River. One day it will be as famous as St. Emilion (it already eclipses in thrilling richness many wines from there) once it gets over its shyness.

Even the distributors of WA wines have a reserved attitude to them and it isn't difficult to find the reason. In a nut-shell, the basis for WA's obscurity and under-appreciation is because it produces so little wine. During my hours at the Cafe Royal, I tasted wines from many of the significant WA vineyards and all they amounted to was twenty-one names: Capel Vale, Plantagenet, Selwyn, Leeuwin Estate, Vasse Felix, Cape Mentelle, Iron Horse, Pierro, Frankland, Sandalford, Moss Wood, Alkoomi, Madfish Bay, Howard Park, Devil's Lair, Fifth Leg, Houghton, Cullen, Amberley, Evans & Tate and Goundrey. I guess in all WA can muster around 105 vineyards. And to think, WA is over four and a half times the size of France which has 160,000 individual wine growers and vineyard owners!

But then France is fairly well saturated with vines all over. WA has only its extreme south west sprinkled with vines. Perth, the State capital, has vineyards beyond its suburbs and the other main vineyards stretch down and around the littoral strip which describes a vague rhinoceros-head shape lapped by the Indian Ocean. It consists of five main designated wine areas: Perth Hills, Swan Valley, Coastal Plain, Margaret River and Lower Great Southern.

Why, all sentimentality aside, do I regard these wine areas and their wines so highly? Because of the uncommon richness of the fruit (and balance of tannin and alcohol in the reds) which is marked by an unusual finesse, a lack of the soppiness found in certain other Australian wines, and the decisiveness of the texture. Two such wines, a Cape Mentelle cabernet/merlot and a semillon/sauvignon, were among the two tastiest wines I tasted anywhere in the world in 1997. WA wines are wonderful at accompanying reflective pursuits – reading, writing, music-listening, conversing – as well as possessing the oomph to go with food. Many Aussie wines, seeming so potent and flamboyant when tasted solo, simply turn tail and cry 'Mayday! Mayday!' when there's grub on the plate. I tasted several dozen WA wines at the Cafe Royal, wooded and unwooded chardonnays, sauvignon blancs, pinot noirs, shirazes, cabernet sauvignons, merlots, sparkling bruts, rieslings, semillons, various blends, verdelhos, and even a couple of sweet dessert-style wines, and I could not find a disappointing tipple amongst any of them. The vintages were mostly 97s and 96s, some 95s, the odd 94 and one 93.

What does any vinous explorer reading this book do? Though the odd bottle turns up at the high street wine specialists, we must turn to small wine merchants and restaurants. It is in certain restaurants particularly that one finds wonderful WA bottles: particularly those modern eateries where the chefs rule the roost, not the interior designers. One such is The Square, fairly new, *deux etoiles Michelin*, in the West End of London, just off Bond Street, where, by one of those sweet happenstances which incline the most crusty of wine journalists to consider that perhaps there is an angel looking out for him, I was invited to lunch a few days after my equestrian plod around the Cafe Royal.

I was early. I wanted to get my nose in a book for half-an-hour before my publisher turned up (anything to enhance the impression that I am bookish and worth publishing). The man in the grey suit and restrained tie who seemed to be part of the management team was sympathetic to my request for a glass of white wine to also get my nose into and, most importantly, to wash down the fumes and dust a thirty-minute cycle ride across Town had accumulated in the throat. One is in a dilemma at such times. A *real* author would have turned up at least fifteen minutes late and demanded instant vintage champagne. Did I dare be so unmannerly as to order a bottle of wine without my host being there to choose it? The man in the grey suit and restrained tie, as I dithered about whether to order a glass of the house white, said he had opened a bottle of Leeuwin Estate Chardonnay 1994 yesterday by mistake, recorked it, and would I like a glass of that instead (for the same price as the house white)?

I could have fallen off my chair. It was a vintage of the estate I had been unable to taste at the Aussie wine show and here it was being offered to me, albeit in a possibly over-aerated state; and when it arrived, lush, golden and beckoning in the glass, and I inserted my nose I discovered a wine in perfect condition, with the bouquet of rotting hay and ripe melon, and, when tasted, a silky quaffability yet serious depth of vegetal richness which suggested some kind of new-style Meursault. I had another glass, unable to believe my luck. What was left in the bottle I reserved for my hosts who, when invited to taste the liquid in their glasses (not knowing what it was), were unable to believe, until I revealed the provenance of a wine made behind three deserts on the Indian Ocean, that it was not a remarkably forward specimen of pedigree white burgundy from an unusually ripe vintage.

Western Australia is one side of a coin of which the obverse is surely Bulgaria. There is not a single off-licence or high street wine shop that does not have a Bulgaria wine on its shelf. But who makes them? Is there such a thing as a Bulgarian wine maker?

It was to find the answers to these fundamental questions that one deliciously, almost alienly cold, crisply sun-lit, wind-blown March morning in 1998, having walked my school-bound daughter to the bus stop, I sat at my desk – it was 7.25am precisely I distinctly recall – and let the warmth slowly return to my fingers after my walk. My cosy ever-familiar basement wrapped itself around me ('*Constancy is an evolution of one's living quarters into a thought*' the Russian poet Joseph Brodsky observed).

Today was The Day! Outside, visible through the top of my

sous-terrain window, the sun had turned the grey edifice of St Stephen's church across the road a gentle pink. My cheeks, too, were aglow. Today, in less than two hours, I was set to cycle the short distance to Queens Gate down Kensington Palace Gardens, a doubly incongruous thoroughfare for London in that it is closed to public motor traffic and lined with gilt-golden-gated ambassadorial architectural extravagances of the sort which in another country and in another time would inspire the peasants to storm, to hopefully and finally get some answers to the questions posed above. Today, revolution was in the air! Today, I will at last glimpse the rarest sight in the world of wine: the lesser-spotted *oeneologie Bulgaris*.

Indeed, in my case, it was not so much lesser-spotted as *never* spotted. Bulgarian wine makers are notoriously shy. I have never met one. No-one I talk to has ever met one. Yet we have been guzzling Bulgarian wine for thirty years in the UK. We buy millions of gallons of it and it is on sale *everywhere* (I estimate Sainsbury's customers alone swallowed eight and a half million bottles of the stuff in 1997). Our greatest poets – and I quote from John Heath-Stubbs' *Bulgarian Red* – find it inspirational:

> *'Last night we discussed a bottle*
> *Of red Bulgarian wine – inexpensive,*
> *From the local off-licence,*
> *We found it satisfactory – why not, indeed?*
> *Bulgaria, you know, was Thrace,*
> *From whence the cult of Dionysus*
> *Infiltrated the Hellenic lands.'*

Yes, well. Not a great poem (it doesn't get much tastier as it develops – unlike Bulgarian wine) and that otiose *From* to the whence is unfortunate from a literate man, but it's the only Bulgarian wine poem I can find I'm afraid. Perhaps Mr Heath-Stubbs had more than a single bottle inside him when he wrote it. It would be an easy temptation. Bulgarian wine is not only hugely inexpensive, but gloriously drinkable and, as Mr

Heath-Stubbs notes, lurks locally around every street corner.

All this wealth of wine, then, but no-one ready to admit to making it. What could be the reason? What secret was Bulgaria hiding? Who would not be proud to own up to being of the lineage which made the wine for the Hellenic troops in the Trojan war? You will point out, not unreasonably, that surely all I had to do was fly to the country and visit a winery. But the fact is that although the Bulgarian Wine Guild has four times invited me to visit Bulgaria I have never been able to find time to accept. (I finally did in July 1999 but *that's* a story that will have to wait awhile before being told.) An invitation to the Bulgarian embassy, to taste wine, to be offered the chance to shake the hand of a real live *oeneologie Bulgaris*, was, therefore, irresistible. My excitement was such that I could barely slip on my cycle gloves.

Ten minutes on the bike and I am at the ambassador's door. 'Watch the carpet. It slides,' I am warned as I ascend the curved wooden staircase to the tasting room (wondering if the journey down, after all that wine, might be doubly dangerous). As I enter, several hundred bottles of wine, in serried ranks on white-clothed tables, greet me, open-mouthed. As do several human, male, suited-and-tied representatives of Bulgarian wineries. We exchange the usual pleasantries (me not forgetting, as I have been forewarned, that to nod the head is to indicate disapproval to a Bulgarian, shaking it the way to indicate delight).

And then a red-headed, broad-smiling woman with the disposition of someone hiding a great secret comes up and my day is made. Kapka Georgieva is a wine maker and she is very happy to show me the wines she has made. And so it is, over the next few hours as I gargle and spit, and talk to several people about everything from the nature of the Eastern Orthodox Church to how Bulgarian spinach and feta tartlets differ from the renowned Greek *spannakopita*, I discover the truth about Bulgarian wine.

Why is it so unpretentiously drinkable? Why is it so affordable? Why are its makers so discreet?

The answer to all these questions is the same: because Bulgarian wine is made by women. Well, a goodly proportion of it is anyway. The stuff we drink, a fair bit of it, is made by teams of wine scientists in which women figure greatly and in the winery where Kapka calls the shots, the winery at Russe, there are thirty people involved in making wine, ten of which are women. This sort of ratio of women to men may well make Bulgaria the world leader in non-sexist employment policies where wine is concerned.

No wonder all those suited-and-tied men who front the Bulgarian wineries are so quiet about the wine makers. The front men do the easy bit: chutzpah needed, but no genius required (except, if you want to speak fluent English, the ability and commitment to spend a four year chunk of your secondary education doing *all* your lessons in English). It's the wine making, however, which requires real scientific knowledge and a true, creative approach to putting wines together to make blends and to sensing, a fifth sense really, how a wine will develop from an embryonic swill of grey grape juice in a glass to a full-blown adult wine in a bottle on a shelf many months or even years later.

'Maybe I do have a little ambition to show the men women are better at detail,' says Kapka, a touch shyly, in answer to a question. She is clearly a little unused to questions from Western journalists about men. She has a husband. She has a sixteen-year-old son who plays computers, basketball and football. She hardly needs any lessons in male chauvinism. (Wasn't marriage instituted to ensure its survival?)

But as I sat on one of the embassy's sofas and drank a gorgeous, velvety merlot, I thought not only how wonderfully the little Bulgarian spinach and feta pastries, with their red pepper linings, went so well with the wine, but I realised that I was asking Kapka questions she was not familiar with answering in any language, let alone one foreign to her. Her English is well up to fielding questions about wine, but I'm a man after all, as was the Australian wine consultant, David Wollan, at her left elbow and Ivan Zahaniev, managing director of the Bulgarian Vintners Company, on her right. It was left to Mr Wollan to reveal how the more advanced Bulgarian wineries are now getting wine brains from the new world to advise them on the latest techniques. (Bulgaria also receives generous dollops of development money: Domaine Boyar, one of the country's most successful wine exporters, received a $30-million loan from the European Bank for Reconstruction & Development in 1999.)

Fascinating how the world turns. Here's a woman, a native of the country that was once the Thrace of legend, the country where in the 1970s a royal tomb was excavated to reveal a complete set of wine drinking vessels 4000 years old, a land which gave Menelaus's troops, and brother Agamemnon, the Dutch courage to storm the gates of Troy (and who knows, inspired the idea, after a night of vinous carousing, of that wooden horse), and she's happy to accept consultancy advice about making wine from the new kids on the block, the Aussies, who only stuck their first vines in the ground in the late 1780s and whose classic wines don't go further back than the 1950s.

But that's one of the differences between men and women, I find. Women are always prepared to listen to new ideas. And even let others take the credit for their fruits. It's probably an older tradition than anything you might dig up in Bulgaria.

Or Bordeaux – which is where we must away to now. The very word Bordeaux has some sort of snottiness attached to it. Why is this? Why does it immediately induce the feeling that it represents some kind of hoity-toity class distinction? Is it because Bordeaux was the first region to come up with a class distinction for its vineyards – in 1855?

Richard Cobb in his marvellous book '*Paris and Elsewhere*' – published in 1998 by John Murray at £12.99 – writes that in his experience, which is extraordinarily deep and masterfully fluent, 'the only wholly deplorable people that I have met in France are the Bordelais' but maybe his tongue was in his cheek.

Bordeaux isn't, I find, as nauseatingly snotty as the word *claret*. The very echo of it in the ear, the very resonance of it on the tongue, suggests plums in the mouth and a plum position for the speaker using the word. This might be inverted snobbery were it not for the fact that Bordeaux only becomes claret when it is in the mouth of a certain type of Briton. Not even the tribe which grows the grapes, five respectable varieties plus two oddballs, is permitted to utter the word unscathed. I did once hear a Frenchman use the holy word claret, but he blushed at the sniggering his blatant theft provoked (the pronunciation must balance both syllables equally and not force the sibilant dictatorship of the first over the second); correcting himself only made matters worse. The French drink *bordeaux* (small b note – only the proper noun of the town or the region permits the capital B). We *rosbifs* drink *claret*.

Claret is a word, it is clear, with deep class implications. Is there not a significant difference between a French red and a claret and one's expectations of each? Think about it for a moment. Claret is posh. The use of the word designates a certain behavioural status to the user. Mostly the same word in two different languages results in exactly the same image occurring – as, say, when suffering from toothache in Budapest we ask for a *fogorvos* and a dentist appears – but where symbols and symbolism are concerned we encounter the realm of the pseudo-occult; a wine called claret and one called Bordeaux may be one and the same wine, and indeed are, but cla-ret is a gentlemen's club whereas red bordeaux is a public house (and *bordeaux rouge* is a bordello).

A whole culture is implied in the usage of certain words. Even the nature of the shape the lips and cheeks are compelled to adopt to pronounce symbolic words is significant. Please, then, be in no doubt. Wines which can claim membership of the elite *grands crus classes* are clarets. In spirit, soul, and mannerism they are distinctly *clarets*. They represent British wine merchants most *chic* offerings; apply to them the term *rouges de Bordeaux*, however indisputable this fact of their legal provenance, and you commit a *faux pas* of the same magnitude as hailing a royal duke with a 'what can I do for you, squire?' (The fact that the latter form of demotic address is surely to be preferred is not part of the debate here.)

Did I say five important grapes? They are, in descending order of utility, cabernet sauvignon, merlot, cabernet franc, malbec, and petit verdot; the disfavoured pair, carmenere and bouchet, are, like bereted Frogs on bikes festooned with plaits of garlic, something of an antiquated curiosity nowadays (though carmenere is grown in Chile and, raised properly, can have a devastatingly delightful effect on the taste buds).

Having got that out of the way the next question is why claret anyway? Where did the word come from?

The word claret is part of a distinguished cluster of hybrids which, for reasons to do with the stiffness of the British upper lip preventing correct enunciation, also includes hock and sherry. This latter, derived as it is from the town of Jerez (pronounced herr-reth), also has many of the symbolic connotations of claret.

Claret was once *clairet*. This referred, eons ago, to the nature of the red wine then emanating from what was, as Aquitane, a province of the English crown; the wine was, so historians reckon, a moody pink, or light red. *Clairet* can refer in French to a thin gruel or even a high-pitched, reedy, voice; thus we may infer from this that the wine in those days was light, not the depth of rich red it is nowadays, and this was due to the comparatively short time the skins of the grapes were in contact with the juice and so the colour, which comes almost exclusively from the grape skins, was less intense than it is nowadays where extraction times are longer. It was the advances made in the science of wine making and low-yield grape growing by the most famous Medoc chateaux some 250 years ago which led to the deeper richer wines of legend; wines whose reputation today affects (one might say infects) all wines which can call themselves clarets. We can, of course, only guess at what our forefathers and mothers in those far off days precisely experienced from vintage to vintage as they glugged their clarets, though we certainly do know the narrowness of the wine drinking habit which was the sole preserve, on anything like a regular basis, of the ruling and leisure class (in which one has to include, in those days when the peasants knew their place, writers).

I apologise again if all this history is boring you (fruity bits follow in the listing sections of the book and if you're getting cheesed off with my prattling why not take this book round to your nearest wine shop and enjoy yourself?). However, it isn't often I stray into such linguistic waters and I must confess the exercise is doing me good. In general, I despise the classification of vineyards by a 150-year-old list which merely protects real estate values. Perhaps its most melancholy result has been the emergence of the phenomenon known as *le deuxieme vin*. This, to the wiliest wine marketeers on the planet (the French), is nothing more than what is known in international brand manageship as range extension. Easy enough when the product is shampoo, but if it is a vineyard composed of a strictly delimited area then how can you extend it? You can't. But you can make wine made at the same chateau and call it something else (but a something else which relies hugely on its relationship to the legendary wine which has given the chateau its reputation).

Thus we have, for example, Le Second Vin de Mouton Rothschild (among several others). This, in its 1994 manifestation, turned up at £29.95 the bottle at the odd high street wine shop and even supermarket.

That wine, jejune as it was, makes a valuable contribution to certain of the points under discussion here. It proves that the magic of an historic name is often a substitute for the liquid in the bottle. Too many *clarets*, for too many years, have been dull companions for the senses, dramatically shrinking the purse yet offering little to swell the throat in return. I would have rather drunk a score of five quid Bulgarian cabernets than spend thirty smackers on that Rothschild wine.

May I suggest we celebrate instead the true hearty clarets – the robust Falstaffian crowd – which Oddbins, Thresher, et al are pleased to offer us. Let us drink them – the wines from the less celebrated Premieres Cotes, Castillon, Blaye, Fronsac etcetera – with their uniquely gruff but caressing tannins, with the sort of dishes which are equally antiquated: rare sides of beef and lamb, game birds (especially pink breasts of duck), venison, pork chops strewn with garlic and herbs, meaty sausages, pink calves liver and kidneys, well-raised old chickens roasted, wild mushroom risottos, bread and cheese.

You may say what an old fart I have become to talk of such things. But even if that is the case I am supremely happy in my farthood. It is a distinguished condition and uniquely English. My grandfather would be proud of me.

Twenty-five years ago I was not a member of the old farts' federation. I was living in Spain. It furthered my wine knowledge (4-pence a litre it cost to fill a plastic bottle with a minimum of four litres from the local shop) and I was a spectator of the slow death of Franco and the – then astonishing – rapid re-birth of democratic though royalist Spain. I am never more happy than when I am in Spain. Or more accurately in this instance as I write, dreaming of it. Jan Morris, in her marvellous book on the country, wrote: 'There is a fanfare to the very name of Spain, and no nation offers an image more vivid. She seems to follow no fashion, obey no norm.'

This was also largely true of the wines (rioja excepted, which aped bordeaux during the forties, fifties and sixties, and even seventies). But nowadays pockets of internationalism have sprung up all over the land, foreign influence in terms of technique and grape variety is everywhere evident, there is a buzz to Spanish wine everywhere. Jerez can be largely excepted from these stirrings; deeply unfashionable wines like Oloroso secco, Mazanilla and Palo Cortado are magnificently *sui generis* (thus beyond bringing into line with modern tastes).

The dizzy rebirth of Spanish wine has been noted by wine commentators, but its deepest effects and significance have not been widely trumpeted. However, to my mind it is an event of earth-shattering moment; the vinous geology of Europe has been deeply altered.

On many major retailers' shelves Spanish wines are now significantly more numerous than Germans.

This overturns hundreds of years of mercantile history. As we approach the end of this century, it tells us something about the shape of the next not only as far as wine is concerned but also in the wider context of the thrilling and richly cosmopolitan Europe our children will inhabit.

For what those figures reveal is not some temporary phenomenon, some whim of vinous fashion, but the deeply felt approach that the new Briton takes to his and her drinking habits. In a nutshell, the writing is heavily on the wall for the sweet, vapid, spineless whites of yesterday; taking their place are reds of character and complexity. Spain is replacing Germany as the great British wine provider, alongside France and Italy. German wine, which for our great-grandparents was valued above the best of French, has had its heyday in the UK and although I am a personal devotee of the wines of certain estates of the Rhine, Moselle, Nahr and the Pfalz, I am aware that very few of my readers, in whatever publication I may write, share this inclination of my palate.

In the past, sherry has always distorted the shape of the picture of Spain's wine imports to the UK. Sherry, not a popular drink any more (although it has slightly increased its sales over the past year), is not considered, erroneously in my view, a table wine in any case, being lumped in with fortified wine as some kind of pre- and post-prandial tipple, not a wine for the mid-meal. There are many reasons for sherry's decline, which began the day Harvey's Bristol Cream's advertising agency suddenly realised, in the seventies, that it was shouting but nobody was hearing, but only one reason needs re-stating here: sherry, like liebfraumilch, is out of step with the times on grounds of taste, health, compatibility with new eating habits, and lifestyle.

The new woman and her new man (dragging somewhat in her well-shod heels) of the nineteen nineties is well aware that sweet wine of any sort is yucky, uncool, sexless, doesn't go with the food she likes, and makes no demands on the mind whereas she has lately discovered that red wine is not fattening, is better for the health especially the blood and the heart, is more versatile with food, and is an infinitely more colourful, sensual, and exciting companion in every situation. If white wine is to be drunk, it should be dry and crisp, like sauvignon blanc, or more buttery, like chardonnay. Germany, on all these counts, simply doesn't get a look in (though it is beginning to try with certain new cheap wines).

Increasingly, however, Spain is getting a look in everywhere you look. There are several reasons for this but the three I will cite here, since they are the most interesting, are these: first, Spain's younger drinkers are turning against the habits of their wine loving elders and so the Spanish wine industry has urgently had to re-equip itself and to export vigorously to survive; second, the exchange rate between the peseta and the pound has been in the UK's favour for some years and will only improve; thirdly, Britons love Spain and regard it as warm and welcoming (unlike other countries which are considered cold and mechanical and although they may churn out solid motor cars, who wants a Volkswagen with gothic number plates on the dinner table?).

Spanish wine, red and white, is flooding onto the shelves of British wine retailers in increasing numbers. For some time we have had splendid Cavas and that terrific sweet dessert wine, Moscatel de Valencia, but now reds and whites from Penedes, Costers del Segre, Navarra, Conca de Barbera, Duero, Toro, Borja, Valdeorras, Somontano, and other areas are pouring in.

It is with these red and white table wines that Spain is flexing new muscles. Of course, we all know about Rioja but wine shop wine buyers are increasingly foraging in areas new to most British drinkers and coming up with some fascinating new wines. Take Rias Baixas. Exactly. Could it be the name of a Basque tennis or *pelota* player? A few years ago only wine scrutineers like me would have given a toss, but professional wine buyers – not just the narrow specialists – are making the long trek out to the region of Galicia, within which the demarcated wine area of Rias Baixas sits, and are coming away with white wines which demonstrate that the British thirst for something different, even if it is a touch expensive, is inexhaustible. Galicia, which sits slightly askew Portugal's head like a crumpled *toque* and juts out scowlingly into the Atlantic, has a grape variety called *albarino*. (Pronounced al-bur-rin-yo since there is a black squiggly thing which squats, like one of the region's rain clouds, above the n.) Unusually vibrant, with a hint of spice and a touch of vegetality, and with delightfully uncertain acidity, this is a quirky glugging wine as well as one which will go with a whole range of fish and seafood dishes.

Why is Spain being so generous with its home-grown treasures? It has no choice but to yield them to an export market. It was a philosophical wine producer in Valdeorras – when I finally did get off my butt late last year and visit Spain – who pointed out to me that twenty years ago the locals drank around 60 litres of wine per capita per year. The figure today, he told me, is somewhere around the middle 30s. But the grapes are still being grown. The vineyards, in some cases, are being expanded. The resultant wine, as with so many other vineyard regions in Spain, is ending up in the UK.

Even Jan Morris, one of the most rewarding travel writers to ever unpack her predilections, might be surprised at this new outward looking energy. Indeed, there is no more delicious way to appreciate her limpidly witty yet authoritative style than with a copy of her beautifully written Penguin paperback on the country along with which you have also opened a bottle of Marques de Grinon Valdepusa Syrah. Grown near Toledo (the former home of Europe's finest blades), this glorious wine is proof that Spain can make intensely fruity reds of the highest possible class which don't come from Rioja or from long established influences like the regal Miguel Torres in Catalonia. This syrah is dry, spicy, savoury, balanced, rich and very, very deep, and has hugely lingering flavours. An exciting wine, uniquely Spanish – which is to say, bearing in mind Jan Morris's observation I started with, like no other wine you have ever put your lips to: gutsy, with lots of bravura fruit, but very smooth and civilised.

All right, so it costs around a tenner at its various outlets. But the occasional indulgence is permitted, no? Let's drink to the future. It is red and it is Spanish.

It is also Italian. Italy has always dragged in other's heels where commercial exploitation of a natural resource is concerned because Italians are lazy business people on their home soil. This is especially true where wine is concerned. But even in the region of the Eternal City things are changing.

Rome not only drinks Frascati, it eats Frascati. Since the time of Nero (slight exaggeration, but certainly for a long time) Frascati has been known as the 'house wine' of Rome and over the past ten years this has become literally true. More than a thousand acres of Frascati vines in that time have been sacrificed to make way for the building of new homes and the latest project is the construction of a whole new university town, Torvergata by name, on 400 acres of ex-Frascati vineyards. As you pass by the site it seems as if a Latin convention of cranes is being held and surely every crane in Italy has been put up for it (and one feels that up there somewhere surely there lurks, wrench in hand, Primo Levi's heroic fictional engineering rigger, Libertino Faussone).

I have been itching to write about Italian wines for some time ever since I came across some bottles of 1994 Zenato Valpolicello Classico Superiore Ripasso in a local shop. Licking my lips in disbelief (since I had been completely unaware of its proximity to my thirst), I liberated every bottle from the store cheerfully forking out £7.29 for each one. The wine was then served at my wife's Very Special Birthday Party where it partnered roast rump of lamb; a marriage which the guests, who had had little prior experience of Valpolicella in such noble form, pronounced astonishing and delicious: for this Valpol is not remotely like the gunge we all know and loathe from our first experience of drinking it in an Italian restaurant in Britain. For most of us, I daresay that bottle is to be remembered with all the scant affection with which we recall out first sexual kiss. But this Zenato Ripasso is something else: Zenato refers to the name of a great wine maker, Ripasso to a process of production peculiar to the area of Verona where the wine comes from. This involves passing the fresh wine over all the bits and bobs of skins and pips left over from a wine made the previous year from dried grapes. This gives an added depth and subtlety to the wine, and promotes the development of almond, bitter cherry, chocolate and other rich flavourings. The wine is very fruity but also dry – dry in a uniquely Ripasso way. It is a fabulous food wine, such is its extravagance; yet, at the same time, it has a voluptuous elegance.

Inspired by these experiences and in the knowledge that 1997 was, in one Italian wine maker's words 'the best for fifty years in the whole of Italy – not a drop of rain anywhere in the period leading up to and during the harvest', I went off to Italy in summer 1998 to see for myself what was happening to the world's second largest wine-grape grower (after France). In Frascati, this has to include a visit to Frascati's largest grower, Fontana Candida (which was actually the first Italian wine I ever tasted at a British Italian restaurant but unlike that first kiss the memory of the wine has lasted better, perhaps because it was the more successful occurrence). Naturally, it was the 1997 wines I tasted first, young and keen and full of themselves, but even then they managed to spring an even more modern surprise.

This was because of the influence, in certain examples, of Australian wine maker Geoff Merrill. The idea of an Aussie having a say in Frascati is something like discovering bagpipes made in Osaka – well, yes, of course it's *possible* but is it remotely the real thing? You may say, bearing in mind how much filth has flaunted the Frascati name in the past, that surely this is only to the good but Fontana Candida's has always been a benchmark Frascati and Mr Merrill's example of it, bearing a supermarket own-label, is beyond reproach. It differs from traditional Frascastis, however, in that the wine has not been permitted to undergo any degree of malolactic fermentation.

This ferment, secondary to the alcoholic one where yeasts transform the sugars into alcohol, changes the chemical nature of a wine's acidity from malic (appley and keen) to lactic (milky and soft). A Japanese bagpipe indeed, but one we barbarians south of the border will surely find unusually melodious.

After a rapid sandwich lunch in the tasting room (remarkable for its ingenious Italian engineered fully plumbed-in individual ceramic spitoons which slide out from drawers concealed beneath the edge of the large round conference table), it was on the road again to visit Orvieto, built on an old Etruscan outcrop ninety miles north in Umbria. Most impressive here was again Aussie influenced wine, made from the local sangiovese grape. The sangiovese grape is of course the great chianti grape but in this Orvieto it was more exciting than your average chianti because although it is fresh and juicy, with barely a hint of chianti's earthiness, the aroma is deeper, there is a superbly rich and energetic backbone to the fruit, and the tannins are alert and graceful. It would, I felt, develop well for 2 or 3 more years yet, but it was also excellent now – especially with food. Indeed, so impressed with this wine was I that I insisted on taking the bottle I had tasted in the tasting room to dinner with me some hours later.

This dinner, at the *il Giglio d'oro* restaurant in Orvieto's main square where the dominant theme is the horizontally striped stone work of the Romanesque-Gothic cathedral (a melancholy edifice to regard as the sun slides away and the crepuscular square hosts a performance of strolling shadows, clacking heels on cobble stones, the odd perambulating prelate smug and smiling, and the shouts of children), could have been cooked specifically for the Merrill sangiovese so deeply did the wine and food agree. The wine never wavered once even with risotto with pancetta and local rabbit drenched in aromatic herbs for company.

Next morning I faced the stiff drive to Verona (some 350 miles north west) but my driver was veteran wine maker Carlo Corino, so there was plenty to talk about, and the big BMW took just four hours to eat up the miles and deposit us outside the offices of Italy's newest wine exporting company, Arcadia (one full-time employee in Frederica Nenz), in Verona. I took off my jacket, rolled up my sleeves, and began the daily ritual of sniffing, swirling, slurping and spitting. Well, it was only 26 wines. Barely enough to give a chap an appetite for lunch (which I had not yet had).

Here were Soaves, pinot grigios, Bardolinos, Valpolicellas, Barberas, Amarones and Chardonnay/Garganega blends. These last were a touch raw but would improve in bottle. As I muttered aloud along these lines, Carlo chipped in with 'I can't live with a wine which won't improve and will be less good in twelve months. I can't sleep at night.' It was the Amarone, though, which I elected to more deeply research over dinner. Carlo refers to this wine as one of those local masterpieces which are 'vini di meditazione'. That is to say a wine to think about, to mull over; a wine to set you meditating on the pleasures of life.

My meditating went along these lines: Italy is a vast treasure house of buried wine riches it requires only a map and loose command of the language to dig up. Here was a small British wine importer, Arcadia, only a year old, off-spring of the well-established Enotria company based in north London, and yet it already had, in as short a time as eighteen months or less, a range of wines which would set surging the saliva of any major wine retailer in the UK – along with a delightful disturbance to the pocket which shows that there are bargains to be had. Italy is a hopeless exporter of its wines on any skilfully marketed scale. Its UK trade office, compared with the French, is feeble and undynamic and this is surely representative of the attitude of its paymasters back in Italy.

Italy has had it soft for so long, perhaps because it can rely on so many Italian restaurateurs to eagerly purchase its products, that it has never developed any coherent trade policy with other aspects of the UK wine scene. It is noticeable, to any sensitive observer, that at any international wine fair it is the Italian stands which are left unattended at lunch times, that its representatives think nothing of lighting up during working hours and spreading tobacco fumes to mingle with the flavours of its wines, and that there is a relaxed, almost take-it-or-leave-it attitude with many Italian exporters. (I strongly except from this censure exemplary dynamos of industry and eloquence like Stephano Girelli, and a very few others, who have developed fantastic relationships with major UK wine retailers.)

Well, who cares? This is a wine guide, not an economic review or a submission document to an export board. But the reader may find it is illuminating in passing to consider that it is so relatively easy for a new company to so rapidly make significant inroads into the world's second largest wine producing country. Indeed, it is heartening, for us UK drinkers, that it is. Mr Mark Kermode, the Enotria executive responsible for much of the dynamism behind its Arcadia subsidiary, is not only a brilliant speaker of Italian (his mastery of Roman gutter slang is such that he is received as a God in humbler cities of the peninsula and the Sicilian isles), but a richly endowed salesman who could, were he as sly as Iago and as ambitious as Richard Gloucester, become Master of all Italy. It is a measure of his charm and modesty that he will be embarrassed to read this – though all I wish to do is to urge him and Arcadia on to greater heights.

My interest is my readers' interests: terrific wines as cheap as they can be. If Italy can offer this, as do Spain and Bulgaria, then the road of my life is more smoothly paved. I may even find some time to get out and about more. Though after my comments above, there may not be a queue of Italian exporters thrilled to invite me.

Health Warning!

Health Warning is an arresting phrase. I hope by employing it I may save you from working yourself up into a state. Let me explain.

I get a few letters a week from readers (both column and

book) telling me that a wine which I have said is on sale in a certain off-licence is not there and that the wine has either sold out or the branch claims to have no knowledge of it; I get letters telling me that a wine is a bit dearer than I said it was; and I get the odd note revealing that the vintage of the 16-point wine I have enthused about and which my correspondent desperately wants to buy is different from the one listed.

First of all, let me say that no wine guide in the short and inglorious history of the genre is more exhaustively researched, checked, and double-checked than this one. I do not list a wine if I do not have assurances from its retailer that it will be widely on sale when the guide is published. Where a wine is on restricted distribution, or stocks are short and vulnerable to the assault of determined readers (i.e. virtually all high rating, very cheap bottles), I will always clearly say so. However, large retailers use computer systems which cannot anticipate uncommon demand and which often miss the odd branch off the anticipated stocking list. I cannot check every branch myself (though I do nose around them when I can) and so a wine in this book may well, infuriatingly, be missing at the odd branch of its retailer and may not even be heard of by the branch simply because of inhuman error. Conversely, the same technology often tells a retailer's head office that a wine is out of stock when it has merely been completed cleared out of the warehouse. It may still be on sale in certain branches. Then there is the fact that not every wine I write about is stocked by every single branch of its listed retailer. Every store has what are called retail plans and there may be half-a-dozen of these and every wine is subject to a different stocking policy according to the dictates of these cold-hearted plans.

I accept a wine as being in healthy distribution if several hundred branches, all over the country not just in selected parts of it, stock the wine. Do not assume, however, that this means every single branch has the wine.

I cannot, equally, guarantee that every wine in this book will still be in the same price band as printed (these bands follow this introduction). The vast majority will be. But there will always be the odd bottle from a country suddenly subject to a vicious swing in currency rates, or subject to an unprecedented rise in production costs which the supermarket cannot or is not prepared to swallow, and so a few pennies will get added to the price. If it is pounds, then you have cause for legitimate grievance. Please write to me. But don't lose a night's sleep if a wine is twenty pence more than I said it is. If you must, write to the appropriate wine shop chain. The department and the address to write to are provided with each entry.

Now the puzzle of differing vintages. When I list and rate a wine, I do so only for the vintage stated. Any other vintage is a different wine requiring a new rating. Where vintages do have little difference in fruit quality, and more than a single vintage is on sale, then I say this clearly. If two vintages are on sale, and vary in quality and/or style, then they will be separately rated. However, be aware of one thing.

Streetplonk sells a fair number of copies. I say this not to brag but, importantly, to acquaint you with a reality which may cause you some irritation. When *Streetplonk* appears on sale there will be lots of eager drinkers aiming straight for the highest rating wines as soon as possible after the book is published. Thus the wine buyer who assures me that she has masses of stock of Domaine Piddlewhatsit and the wine will withstand the most virulent of sieges may find her shelves emptying in a tenth of the time she banked on – not knowing, of course, how well I rate the wine until the book goes on sale. It is entirely possible, therefore, that the vintage of a highly rated wine may sell out so quickly that new stocks of the follow-on vintage may be urgently brought on to shelf before I have tasted them. This can happen in some instances. I offer a bunch of perishable pansies, not a wreath of immortelles. I can do nothing about this fact of wine writing life, except to give up writing about wine.

Lastly, one thing more:

'*Wine is a hostage to several fortunes (weather being even more uncertain and unpredictable than exchange rates) but the wine writer is hostage to just one: he cannot pour for his readers precisely the same wine as he poured for himself.'*

This holds true for every wine in this book and every wine I will write about in the years to come (for as long as my liver holds out). I am sent wines to taste regularly and I attend wine tastings all the time. If a wine is corked on these occasions, that is to say in poor condition because it has been tainted by the tree bark which is its seal, then it is not a problem for a bottle in decent condition to be quickly supplied for me to taste. This is not, alas, a luxury which can be extended to my readers.

So if you find a wine not to your taste because it seems pretty foul or 'off' in some way, then do not assume that my rating system is up the creek; you may take it that the wine is faulty and must be returned as soon as possible to its retailer. Every retailer in this book is pledged to provide an instant refund for any faulty wine returned – no questions asked. I am not asking readers to share all my tastes in wine, or to agree completely with every rating for every wine. But where a wine I have well rated is obviously and patently foul then it is a duff bottle and you should be compensated by getting a fresh bottle free or by being given a refund.

How I Rate a Wine

Value for money is my single unwavering focus. I drink with my readers' pockets in my mouth. I do not see the necessity of paying a lot for a bottle of everyday drinking wine and only rarely do I consider it worth paying a high price for, say, a wine for a special occasion or because you want to experience what a so-called 'grand' wine may be like. There is more codswallop talked and written about wine, especially the so-called 'grand' stuff, than any subject except sex. The stench of this gobbledegook regularly perfumes wine merchants' catalogues, spices the backs of bottles, and rancidises the writings of those infatuated by or in the pay of producers of a particular wine region. I do taste expensive wines regularly. I do not, regularly, find them worth the money. That said, there are some pricey bottles in these pages. They are here either because I wish to provide an accurate, but low, rating of its worth so that readers will be given pause for thought or because the wine is genuinely worth every penny. A wine of magnificent complexity, thrilling fruit, superb aroma, great depth and finesse is worth drinking. I would not expect it to be an inexpensive bottle. I will rate it highly. I wish all wines which commanded such high prices were so well deserving of an equally high rating. The thing is, of course, that many bottles of wine I taste do have finesse and depth but do not come attached to an absurdly high price tag. These are the bottles I prize most. As, I hope, you will.

20 Is outstanding and faultless in all departments: smell, taste and finish in the throat. Worth the price, even if you have to take out a second mortgage.

19 A superb wine. Almost perfect and well worth the expense (if it is an expensive bottle).

18 An excellent wine but lacking that ineffable sublimity of richness and complexity to achieve the very highest rating. But superb drinking and thundering good value.

17 An exciting, well-made wine at an affordable price which offers real glimpses of multi-layered richness.

16 Very good wine indeed. Good enough for *any* dinner party. Not expensive but terrifically drinkable, satisfying and multi-dimensional – properly balanced.

15 For the money, a good mouthful with real style. Good flavour and fruit without costing a packet.

14 The top end of the everyday drinking wine. Well-made and to be seriously recommended at the price.

13 Good wine, true to its grape(s). Not great, but very drinkable.

12 Everyday drinking wine at a sensible price. Not exciting, but worthy.

11 Drinkable, but not a wine to dwell on. You don't wed a wine like this, though you might take it behind the bike shed with a bag of fish and chips.

10 Average wine (at a low price), yet still just about a passable mouthful. Also, wines which are terribly expensive and, though drinkable, cannot justify their high price.

9 Cheap plonk. Just about fit for parties in dustbin-sized dispensers.

8 On the rough side here.

7 Good for pickling onions or cleaning false teeth.

6 Hardly drinkable except on an icy night by a raging bonfire.

5 Wine with more defects than delights.

4 Not good at any price.

3 Barely drinkable.

2 Seriously – did this wine come from grapes?

1 The utter pits. The producer should be slung in prison.

The rating system above can be broken down into six broad sections.

Zero to 10: Avoid – unless entertaining stuffy wine writer.

10, 11: Nothing poisonous but, though drinkable, rather dull.

12, 13: Above average, interestingly made. Solid rather than sensational.

14, 15, 16:   This is the exceptional, hugely drinkable stuff, from the very good to the brilliant.

17, 18:   Really wonderful wine worth anyone's money: complex, rich, exciting.

19, 20:   A toweringly brilliant world-class wine of self-evident style and individuality.

Prices

It is impossible to guarantee the price of any wine in this guide. This is why instead of printing the shop price, each wine is given a price band. This attempts to eliminate the problem of printing the wrong price for a wine. This can occur for all the usual boring but understandable reasons: inflation, economic conditions overseas, the narrow margins on some supermarket wines making it difficult to maintain consistent prices and, of course, the existence of those freebooters at the Exchequer who are liable to inflate taxes which the supermarkets cannot help but pass on. But even price banding is not foolproof. A wine listed in the book at, say, a B band price might be on sale at a C band price. How? Because a wine close to but under, say, £3.50 in spring when I tasted it might sneak across the border in summer. It happens, rarely enough not to concern me overmuch, but wine is an agricultural import, a sophisticated liquid food, and that makes it volatile where price is concerned. Frankly, I admire the way retailers have kept prices so stable for so many years. We drink cheaper (and healthier) wine now than we did thirty years ago. The price banding code assigned to each wine works as follows:

Price Band

A Under £2.50   B £2.50 to £3.50   C £3.50 to £5

D £5 to £7   E £7 to £10   F £10 to £13

G £13 to £20   H Over £20

All wines costing under £5 (i.e. A–C) have their price band set against a black background.

ACKNOWLEDGEMENTS

I must doubly acknowledge the input of Ben Cooper in the preparation of this book; last year, his name was left off these acknowledgements when it would be quite impossible for me to write an accurate word about some of the behind-the-scenes goings-on at retailers but for Mr Cooper's assiduous research. I thank him – doubly. Linda Peskin, whose unquenchable flame burns brightly into every crevice of this little book, is also to be acknowledged for it is she who assists me in running all the computer software systems necessary to compile, check, recheck, and list in sensible order all the wines I taste. Sheila Crowley, Kate Lyall Grant, Jamie Hodder-Williams, Martin Neild, Karen Geary, and Diane Rowley, to whom this book is dedicated, at my publisher are also to be thanked. I would also like to thank Michael Wynn Jones, the delightful editor of Sainsbury's Magazine, who originally published, during 1998 and in various different forms, some of the introduction to this book. As ever, I am grateful I fell into the delightful arms of Felicity Rubinstein and Sarah Lutyens, literary agents, after my previous disillusioning experiences at the hands of this secret, percentaged branch of literature.

FULLERS

In the middle of last year, this London and home counties based retailer (and splendid brewer) announced bold expansion plans for its chain of off-licences. It is aiming to grow to 80 shops over the next five years. However, there will be pain before gain as some of the smaller shops in the chain are likely to close in the short term. Up to 1998, the net size of the chain had fallen from 69 to 64 branches, hardly a severe pruning, but profits had risen by 51% to £1.5 million (according to a report in *Off-Licence News*). The company said it was also considering opening some sort of warehouse-style shop following examples set by Victoria Wine, Parisa and Oddbins. It doesn't surprise me. Every high street chain dreams about the same thing and, I have no doubt, even a good few of the more ambitious wine merchants.

Fullers is very much, however, a London-based business (London Pride, its great bitter, is a national treasure) and warehouse space comes at a premium. The company seems, not unreasonably, to be taking geographical expansion very cautiously. 'We wouldn't open up in Birmingham at this stage,' managing director, Michael Turner told *Off-Licence News* in June 1998. This is not to be viewed as a slight on the good burghers (and boozers) of Britain's second city but relates to logistics. Brewers are highly traditional animals with caution built-in as thick and protective as tortoise shell. Fullers can, for example, easily contemplate expanding west from London because it already has trucks delivering to pubs in that direction but I don't see it going north or east.

By December 1998, the Fullers wine shop estate had shrunk

further to 61 stores but the company was still sticking to its aim of getting up to 80 stores. How curious, as Alice might have remarked, that I seem to be getting smaller when I thought my intention was to grow bigger. 'It's a question,' said Mr Turner, 'of finding the right sites.'

Six-month profits from the off-licence division did not shrink, though. They had increased by 11%, with like-for-like sales and margins also improving, the company reported. A further boost was doubtless provided in 1998 when Fullers won the Regional Chain of the Year award at the highly silly International Wine Challenge. This was their third straight win in a row so presumably the chain gets to keep the cup (or whatever it is – most likely a pompous certificate heavily signatured which can be framed and stuck where it can be ignored by all sensible people).

More interesting (and certainly more insightful) is the Community Service Award which Stuart Roberts, the deputy manager of the Fullers store at Youngs Corner in Hammersmith, ought to be up for. Last August, this store was robbed but the wretched perpetrator was in the dark as to Mr Roberts' artistic talents. Mr Roberts does, apparently, sketch people sitting opposite him on the tube going home (a risky occupation I would have thought – Mr Roberts is patently a brave artist) and his in-store displays are reputed to be works of art. He was able to sketch the miscreant for the police who found it matched the description of someone already under suspicion. The suspect was immediately put under surveillance. I am unaware if Mr Roberts has ever had an exhibition of his work but if this case ever goes to court he can, one assumes, feel confident that at least one of his works will be an exhibit.

I picked up this story from 'The Griffin', the Fuller Smith & Turner (Fullers' full name) internal newspaper, in which Fullers wine buyer, Roger Higgs, has a regular column. Mr Higgs is a game chap. He has been pictured on these pages wearing a balaclava, a Ruud Gullit wig and dressed as Santa Claus. However, via a profile on young Rodge in *Off-Licence*

News, it was revealed that he doesn't write his column himself. Who does write it? I have no idea. I forgot to ask him last time I saw him. (It may be Mr Oz Clarke. Ghost writing is surely not beyond his manifold talents and he also lives, if he hasn't moved since I last looked, locally to the brewery.) In the interview, Mr Higgs gave his views on what off-licences had to do to compete with supermarkets now that the latter have improved their wine ranges so dramatically and so competitively. In Mr Higgs' view, the specialist chains have to be just that: special. It is not enough to have a range of good wines; the supermarkets already do that. Off-licence chains, especially bijou ones like Fullers, can set themselves apart by offering wines that the supermarkets and even the larger off-licence groups cannot carry, those that are in such limited quantities that it would simply not be viable for them. I am frequently told by supermarkets that certain wines are only available in selected stores and I regularly receive letters from frustrated readers telling me that a wine I reviewed was not available at their local store (even though I always inform readers of such limited distribution and I offer the advice to always phone the local branch before travelling). This, Mr Higgs informs us, is far less likely to happen with a small off-licence chain. Lacking the buying power of the big boys, Mr Higgs believes that companies like Fullers have to concentrate on the higher price points. He says Fullers is working especially hard in the £5 to £8 segment though he does not wish to give us the idea that Fullers is not competitive around £3.99. I would comment that it is certainly in the £5 to £8 where Fullers is strongest. The £3.99 area, certain specimens excepted, is rapidly being ruled out of court for the smaller chains because the best wines around this price are so well-priced precisely because of the huge buying clout of the supermarkets. In any case, Fullers should not try to be competitive in the cheaper area because it will fail to find enough wines within it which are worthy of their shops. This is no bad thing. I believe strongly that far from driving chains like Fullers out of business, the supermarkets have encouraged drinkers to experiment and so this chain can prosper and get fatter, if, as Mr Higgs has amply demonstrated in the past, the over-a-fiver wines are still great value for money.

In this context, I would warmly recommend young Roger's Languedoc reds, the Pic Saint Loup crowd especially. They represent splendid tippling and they are exactly the sort of complex, tannic, exciting wines upon which Fullers needs to concentrate. Roger – no more talk of £3.99 wines, please (bargain offers to get rid of stock apart, that is).

Fuller Smith & Turner plc
Griffin Brewery
Chiswick Lane South
London W4 2BQ
Tel: 0181 996 2000
Fax: 0181 995 0230

SEE STOP PRESS SECTION AT END OF BOOK FOR LAST-MINUTE ADDITIONS OR UPDATES TO THIS RETAILER'S RANGE.

ARGENTINIAN WINE RED

Alianza Malbec Maipu 1997 | 13.5 | C

Alianza Merlot Maipu 1997 | 12 | C

Balbi Shiraz 1997 | 16 | C

Starts babyish (and soft and lip-smackingly fruity) then goes dry, earthy and serious. Impactful stuff of charismatic charms.

Bonarda Tempranillo, J & F Lurton 1997 | 12.5 | C

Bright Bros Argentine Red NV | 13 | B

Catena Malbec Lunluntu Vineyard 1995 | 16 | E

Baked fruit, warm tannin, fur-coat thick texture. A real Christmas wine!

Gran Lurton Cabernet Sauvignon 1997 | 15.5 | E

Massive juicy attacking fruit style with loads of tannins. Great with food.

Norton Cabernet 1997 | 16.5 | C

Tobacco, touch of chocolate, hint of cassis. Enough excitement for any glass.

Norton Malbec 1996 | 16 | C

Meaty yet dry, rich yet deft, this has loads of flavour yet finesse. A plump paradox of a wine.

Norton Privada 1996   `14` `E`

Very drinkable but I can't quite see why it costs eight quid.

Syrah J & F Lurton 1998   `16` `C`

Terrific dryness, Rhone style, but with rich cherry-edged fruit. Outstanding quaffing here.

Trivento Syrah 1998   `16.5` `C`

Absolutely fantastic texture and savoury richness here. Superb tannins and tenacity.

ARGENTINIAN WINE   WHITE

Alamos Ridge Chardonnay 1996   `16` `C`

Brilliant value here: such calm, such elegant fruitiness.

Bright Brothers Argentine White NV   `14` `B`

Soft yet crisp, dry yet fruity, eager yet restrained. A simple glugging bargain.

Catena Chardonnay 1996   `E`

Very elegant, tongue stretching fruit which lingers most entertainingly. It has an ineffable purity to it.

La Rural Pinot Blanc 1998   `C`

Superbly polished and plummy textured wine of great class and conviction.

AUSTRALIAN WINE   RED

**Clancy's Red Shiraz/Cabernet Sauvignon/
Merlot/Cabernet Franc 1996**   `14.5` `E`

A very potent broth of soft, ripe, meaty fruit which requires food
to be acceptable. Indian food, casseroles, Spanish/Portuguese
stews etc., you know the sort of thing.

**Four Sisters Grenache Shiraz, McLaren
Vale 1996**   `13` `D`

Grant Burge Old Vine Shiraz 1997   `14` `E`

Shiraz, like raita, as an accompaniment to Indian food.

Hardys Bankside Shiraz 1996   `14` `D`

Hardys Banrock Station Shiraz 1997   `15.5` `D`

It's the fresh young edge which makes it so classic. Has a coal-tar
syrah ripeness of the Rhone.

**Hardys Nottage Hill Cabernet Sauvignon/
Shiraz 1998**   `16` `D`

Loads of savoury plums and blackberries with lovely earthy
tannins. Scrumptious drinking here.

Jamiesons Run Reserve Coonawarra 1996   `12` `G`

Gawky, overpriced, eccentric.

Leasingham Grenache 1996 `15.5` `E`

This is improving nicely in bottle. Terrific sweet/rich, soft/hard, juicy/dry grenache.

Lindemans Bin 45 Cabernet Sauvignon 1997 `14.5` `D`

More correct than exciting but well-formed and rich to finish. Good with food.

Lindemans Cawarra Dry Red 1997 `14` `C`

About as dry as Oz gets at this price.

Madfish Bay Pinot Noir 1997 `10` `E`

Tastes like the meat's already been marinaded in it.

Mount Langi Ghiran Shiraz 1996 `10` `G`

Penfolds Bin 35 Cabernet Sauvignon/ Shiraz/Ruby Cabernet 1997 `14` `D`

Juicy and well-meaning.

Rockford Grenache 1996 `13` `E`

Fruit juice.

Rosemount Estate Cabernet Sauvignon 1998 `15` `E`

Very juicy and ripe and with a lovely warm but subtle tannic underbelly. It purrs like a cat.

Rosemount Estate Shiraz 1998 `14.5` `E`

In the Rosemount tradition of juice with an adult attitude. Totally quaffable.

Shadrach Barossa Valley Cabernet 1993 [11] [G]

Yes, of course you'd accept a glass and murmur 'how nice'. But eighteen quid to buy! No way, Jose.

Tyrrell's Eclipse Pinot Noir 1996 [11] [E]

AUSTRALIAN WINE · WHITE

Banrock Station Chardonnay 1998 [12] [C]

Very sticky and uncomfortable.

Grant Burge Late Picked Dry Muscat 1998 [16] [C]

Wonderful, rich, semi-dry, spicy fruit. Great with Peking duck.

Green Point Chardonnay 1996 [13.5] [E]

Ironstone Semillon Chardonnay 1998 [16] [D]

Really handsome, quality quaffing. Has pizzazz, personality, dryness yet richness. Also suits loads of fish dishes.

Katnook Sauvignon, Coonawarra 1998 [16] [E]

Superb depth and length with angular fruit of immense class and savour. It has a rich complexity and fruit harnessed to fine acids. A lovely wine.

Lindemans Bin 70 Semillon/Verdelho/ Sauvignon Blanc/Chardonnay 1997 [15] [D]

Brilliant soft spiciness for oriental food.

Lindemans Coonawarra Botrytis Riesling
1996 (half bottle) `17` `D`

Magnificently alluring bouquet suggestive of spiced soft fruit.
Thereafter it's like an eccentric Trockenbeerenauslese of unusual
ripeness and limpidity.

Lindemans Limestone Coast Chardonnay
1997 `16` `D`

Full of personality, polish, plumpness and poise. Lovely stuff.

Madfish Bay Chardonnay 1997 `16` `E`

Not typically Aussie – no oil or nuts or spicy melon – but you
do get freshness, finesse, firmness and a fine sense of high quality
grapes singing in unison.

Peter Lehmann Barossa Semillon 1998 `14` `D`

Fish wine.

Rawsons Retreat Bin 21 Semillon/
Chardonnay/Colombard 1998 `15` `C`

Fat and full of fun. Great striding style of behaviour over the
taste buds.

Rosemount Chardonnay 1998 `15.5` `D`

Always one of Australia's most accomplished chardonnays. Class
and composure, fluency and flavour.

BULGARIAN WINE   RED

Stony River Bulgarian Red NV `10` `B`

BULGARIAN WINE   WHITE

Stony River Dry White NV   `13` `B`

'I'm busting my balls trying to find whites under three quid' . . .
It's tough, Roger, I know.

CHILEAN WINE   RED

Casa Lapostolle Cuvee Alexandre
Merlot 1997   `17.5` `F`

The sheer naked hedonistic level of polish on this wine's leather
is simply world class. Won't age much – so drink it before 2000
– with friends and fowls.

Concha y Toro Casillero del Diablo
Merlot 1998   `15.5` `C`

Sheer textured loveliness in a bottle.

Concha y Toro Explorer Pinot Noir 1998   `16` `C`

Oh yes! Under-a-fiver cherry rich, dry, polished, characterful
and cheeky.

Concha y Toro Merlot 1998   `15` `C`

Deliciously sweet and rich, if not typically merlot.

Cono Sur Pinot Noir 1997   `16` `C`

Raunchier than many a Volnay at four times the price. Has great
pongy length and savour. This has improved immeasurably in
bottle since I first tasted it.

49

Errazuriz Merlot El Descanso Estate 1997

Errazuriz Reserve Syrah 1997

Runs away with the imagination – has leather, spice, tobacco, chocolate and cassis. And it's all sprinkled with lively yet warm tannins.

La Palma Gran Reserva Merlot 1997

Materially it's silk and velvet. Spiritually, it has the feel of midnight berries lightly crushed. A gorgeous wine for fireside conversation.

La Palma Reserve Cabernet Merlot 1997

At the height of its leathery, soft pepper and vegetal powers, this beautifully textured and finely wrought wine offers astounding depth. Has concentrated class.

La Palmeria Merlot 1998

It combines that wonderful Chilean double-whammy of food fitness and great, concentrated, complex drinking. Gorgeous stuff.

Luis Felipe Edwards Pupilla Cabernet Sauvignon 1998

One of Chile's most claret-like cabs with its tannins and tenacity. The fruit is savoury, bold, textured and never too ripe. The finish is stylish and assured.

Mont Gras Ninquen Merlot 1996

Valdivieso Malbec 1998

Malbec as smooth and plump as it comes picked.

Vina Porta Reserve Cabernet Unfiltered
1996   16.5   D

At the peak of its maturity, this has cassis and ripe plums as
its keynote but underlying these factors are some rich, ready
tannins. A stylish wine of great class.

CHILEAN WINE   WHITE

Casa Lapostolle Cuvee Alexandre
Chardonnay 1996   17.5   E

It's the lingering stealth of the creamy, nutty finish (roast cobs
on a bed of warm custard) which wins the day. It is sheer class
and very individual. An exciting wine.

Concha y Toro Gewurztraminer 1998   16.5   C

Spicy, lightly rich, elegant, young (but will develop gloriously
in bottle for several years). A terrific fish wine and aperitif.

Errazuriz Reserve Chardonnay 1997   16   D

Utterly hedonistic in its casual fruitiness, the forwardness of the
richness is restrained by the acidity. It is not a gentle wine and
it needs food.

La Palmeria Chardonnay 1998   15   C

Restrained, rich, charming acidity, subtle lemon flavours.

Santa Ines Sauvignon Blanc 1999   16   C

As crisp and as decisively gooseberry-fruited as an old-fashioned
Sancerre in a great vintage.

FRENCH WINE   RED

Bourgogne Pinot Noir Roncevie Domaine Arlaud 1997

Pitiful, really.

Cairanne Domaine de Lameillaud 1998

Sweeter than previous vintages but still the earthy tannins compensate and the texture is superb – a polished wine of wit and substance.

Chateau de Cazeneuve Le Roc de Mates Pic St Loup 1996

Jammy undertones to the ripeness but offset by some handsome tannins. At its peak of drinkability.

Chateau de Cazeneuve Terres Rouge 1997

Simply gushes with flavour and a controlled lushness of tone. Hugely quaffable.

Chateau de l'Euziere Cuvee des Escarboucles 1997

Juicier than previous vintages.

Chateau de Lancyre Coteaux du Languedoc 1998

Spicy cherries and plums, hint of the Midi scrub herbs, touch of bacon – not bad for four quid.

Chateau de Lancyre Grand Cuvee Pic St Loup 1996
16.5   E

Brilliant texture, polished yet characterful, with wonderful tannins attached to rich herby fruit. Superb performer with food. The '97 might have replaced it by the time this book comes out.

Chateau du Trignon Sablet Cotes du Rhone Villages 1997
14.5   D

Savoury ripeness and juiciness here. Belated tannin attack.

Chateau Grand Renouil Canon, Fronsac 1996
16   F

A most distinguished amalgam of leather, cassis, tobacco and rich, earthy, herby tannins. A lovely claret of fine texture and stylish finishing powers.

Chateau Hostens Picant AC Sainte Foy Bordeaux 1996
13.5   E

Chateau Sergant La Lalande de Pomerol 1996
14   E

Chewy tannins, some rich varnish to the fruit.

Crozes Hermitage Petite Ruche, Chapoutier 1997
13   E

Domaine de Grangeneuve Vieille Vignes Coteaux du Tricastin 1997
15

Comfortable tannins, rich, tobacco-edged sweet fruit – the combination makes for great balance.

53

DP2 Bourgogne Pinot Noir 1996

La Ciboise Coteaux de Tricastin, Chapoutier 1997

Very fruity and approachable. The tannins attack way after the fruit has descended.

Les Bateaux Syrah J & F Lurton 1997

Very fresh faced and sharp. Good with light food, but hard to quaff a lot of.

Mas Bruguiere Grande Cuvee Pic St Loup 1996

Terrific tannins here, really soft and rich – great layers – big texture.

Syrah Montagne Noire 1998

Quiet yet confident glugging fruit (plum and a hint of Bovril).

Thierry & Guy Utter Bastard Syrah 1998

Very polished in the mouth, though the finish is all of a piece and doesn't startle or develop new strands of flavour.

Valreas Domaine de la Grande Bellane 1998

Wonderful damson-coloured fruit which stretches, as a flavoured artefact, over the taste buds with huge softness and richness. Hugely civilised, svelte and well tailored.

Wild Pig Reserve Shiraz 1998

The energy of the tannins keeps the fruit in excellent order. Sophisticated swigging here.

FRENCH WINE WHITE

Big Frank's Deep Pink VdP d'Oc 1998

A wine to drink under the warm sun.

**Bourgogne Chardonnay Joseph Bertrand
1997**

**Chateau de Lancyre Pic St Loup Rosé
1998**

Roger Higgs' fourth very good rosé, proving, perhaps, that he
has a nose for such things. Roger?

Chateau Haut Grelot, Bordeaux 1999

Minerals, hay, tension – all ingredients of a terrific shellfish
wine. Even has a hint of the estuary.

Chateau Lacroix Merlot Rosé 1998

An extraordinarily classy, dry, complex rosé. A winter rosé of
great class.

**Coteaux du Layon Domaine de Forges
1996**

Glorious honey and toffees here, even a hint of butterscotch.
Sweet? Nope, can't be having with that word. It's *ambrosial.*
And to be drunk with fresh fruit.

Domaine Arjole Equinoxe 1997

FRENCH WHITE

Domaine de l'Arjiole Cuvee Equinoxe 1997

Curiously crunchy fruit of delicious dimensions (pricey, though).

Josmeyer Pinot Auxerrois 'H' Vieilles Vignes 1996

Intriguing oddity.

Le Pot Muscat Sec VdP d'Oc 1998

A delicate, dry aperitif.

Les Salices Sauvignon VdP d'Oc 1998

Macon Davaye Domaine des Deux Roches 1998

Always an excellent white burgundy, this vintage has outstanding balance and crispness.

Richemont Viognier VdP d'Oc 1998

Sancerre Cuvee Flores, Vincent Pinard 1998

Bit pricey, this one, Roger.

St Veran Domaine des Deux Roches 1998

An exemplary white burgundy at a non-obscene price: vegetal, clean, balanced, classy and brilliant with food.

Terret Sauvignon Domaine des Martin VdP d'Oc 1998

Has a plump edge to its finish belying its crisp commencement. Good food wine.

GERMAN WINE WHITE

**Serrig Herrenberg Riesling Kabinett, Bert
Simon 1997**

Cellar it for five years and a 16-pointer will emerge.

ITALIAN WINE RED

A-Mano Primitivo 1997

Rated as the perfect wine to go with Indian food. Without food,
it rates 15.5.

Avignonesi Rosso 1996

Barbera d'Asti Alasia 1995

Barocco Rosso del Salento 1998

Has a cute bruised fruit edge making it a terrific food wine.
Raisiny and ripe.

Bragnolo Rosso VdT 1995

Pinot Nero Alasia 1997

Tre Uve Ultima 1997

Rich, ready, rampant, very juicy and up for food.

Villa Pigna Colle Lungo Rosse delle Marche 1997 `14.5` `D`

Delicious juicy Italian with food-friendly features plus great quaffing virtues.

Vitiano Falesco 1997 `13` `D`

ITALIAN WINE   WHITE

Carato Chardonnay Barrique, Bidoli 1998 `13` `D`

Mezzo Mondo Chardonnay 1998 `13` `C`

Pecile Sauvignon Blanc 1998 `13.5` `C`

Needs six months in bottle to mature.

Ritratti Pinot Grigio Barrel Fermented 1998 `14.5` `D`

An outstanding pinot grigio: crisp, clean, textured, polished, demurely yet impactfully fruity.

Rosato Veronese Arcadia 1999 `14.5` `C`

Lovely rich fruit which never goes soggy or soppy.

Trulli Dry Muscat 1998 `15.5` `C`

Lovely floral edge, dry as you like it, and not a sissy side in sight. A sophisticated aperitif or to go with minted fish dishes and tomato tarts.

NEW ZEALAND WINE RED

Rippon Pinot Noir 1996 `10` `F`

Sacred Hill Basket Press Cabernet 1996 `12` `E`

Nine quid's worth of juice.

NEW ZEALAND WINE WHITE

**De Redcliffe Mangatawhiri Chardonnay
1996** `14` `E`

Delicious if pricey. Debateable value but in the end the sheer
texture of the fruit gives it its rating.

Hunters Sauvignon, Marlborough 1998 `13.5` `E`

Kim Crawford Unoaked Sauvignon 1998 `14` `D`

Expensive, bit indecisive on the finish, but the initial impact
is interesting. Good with food, where the finish has outside
elements to buttress it.

Oyster Bay Marlborough Chardonnay 1998 `16` `D`

Wonderful restraint yet exuberance of intention: spicy, minerally,
lemony, melony, nutty, balanced.

Riflemans Chardonnay 1997 `14.5` `F`

Barrel fermented, of course, and a very hot, explosive wine it is
with its chewiness and vegetal undertones. Needs food.

PORTUGUESE WINE RED

Esporao Aragones 1996 `13` `D`

Quinto do Crasto Douro Tinto 1996 `14` `D`

SOUTH AFRICAN WINE RED

A Few Good Men Shiraz 1998 `16` `D`

Lovely richness and textured tannicity here. Has a ruggedness yet softness, intelligence and wit, warmth and friendliness. A hugely charming wine – whatever its sex.

Bouchard Finlayson Galpins Peak Pinot Noir 1996 `14` `E`

Cabernet 2000 Darling Cellars 1998 `13.5` `D`

Very juicy. Needs spicy, chillied food with cardamom and coriander.

Clos Malverne Pinotage 1998 `16` `D`

Always one of the Cape's most accomplished pinotages, the '98 is in fine fettle.

Fairview Shiraz 1997 `15.5` `D`

Meaty deliciousness.

Glen Carlou Pinot Noir 1998   13.5   E

The finish is a touch clodhopping but the initial fruit attack is clods of fruit firmly stamping their feet.

Gwendolyn Shiraz/Cabernet Sauvignon 1996   13   E

Hercules Paragon Shiraz 1998   13.5   E

Ilanga Pinotage 1998   13.5   C

Jam, sheer jam (with a hint of tannin).

Jordan Cabernet Sauvignon 1995   13   E

Kumala Reserve Cabernet Sauvignon 1997   17   E

Wonderful one-off marvel of sublime cabernet class: pepper, cheroots, blackberries, tannins – it's got the lot. Plus superb textured richness.

Kumala Reserve Merlot 1998   14   E

Good cigar box perfume, but a bit juicy on the finish.

Millbrook Cinsaut 1998   13   C

Intensely juicy.

Mount Disa Shiraz 1997   16   D

So thick that some tasters have had problems expectorating its gorgeously thick fruit. The '98 might have replaced it by the time this book appears on the shelves.

Pinnacle Cabernet Shiraz 1996   13   D

Spice Route Cabernet Merlot 1998 | 17 | E

Sheer unadulterated richness of such texture and finesse, yet power and depth, the drinker waits as each act unfolds. A dramatic wine of huge class.

Spice Route Pinotage 1998 | 16.5 | E

Is the Spice Route trademark lush texture and compelling, savoury tannins? It seems so. This example simply cudgels the taste buds with riches.

Spice Route Shiraz 1998 | 16 | E

The least tannic and lushly fulfilling of the Spice Route reds. The fruit is soft and ripe and the texture is alive, composite and very sunny with a touch of spice of course.

Vergelegen Mill Race Red Cabernet Merlot 1997 | 14.5 | D

Juicy yet not OTT, it is immensely drinkable, bold and very ripe.

Zevenrivieren Cabernet Sauvignon 1998 | 13 | D

SOUTH AFRICAN WINE WHITE

Birdfield Chardonnay 1998 | 13 | B

Bit weak on the finish.

Blauwklippen Chardonnay 1998 | 12 | C

Cathedral Cellar Chardonnay 1997 | 13.5 | E

Coast Line Chenin Blanc 1998 `15` `B`

Good richness, never OTT, dry yet double layers of fruit.
Great price.

Glen Carlou Chardonnay 1998 `15.5` `E`

Lots of richness and roustabout fruitiness here yet it finally
comes clean and cool and finishes with some style.

Jordan Barrel Fermented Chenin 1997 `13` `D`

Jordan Chardonnay, Stellenbosch 1997 `15` `E`

Big chewy white burgundy taste-alike. Great wine for chicken
and posh sea-food dishes.

Louisvale Chardonnay, Stellenbosch 1997 `15` `D`

Lovely soft ripe fruit with a clean pineapple and citrus finish.

Vergelegen Chardonnay 1998 `14` `D`

Elegant, easy-going fruit.

Zevenrivieren Chardonnay 1998 `14` `D`

Rather saucy.

SPANISH WINE RED

Abadia Retuerta 1996 `14` `F`

Very juicy, this vintage.

Berberana Reserva Rioja 1994　　　13　D

Castillo Perelada Cabernet Sauvignon 1995　12.5　D

Very sweet.

Espiral Tempranillo Cabernet 1997　　14　C

Very juicy and Oriental food friendly.

Fuente del Ritmo Tempranillo La Mancha 1996　　15.5　C

Marques de Grinon Dominio de Valdepusa Syrah 1995　　15.5　E

Nekeas Tempranillo/Merlot 1998　　14　C

Very savoury and soupy yet dry to finish.

Vina Albali Gran Reserva 1991　　16　D

Terrific char-grilled animal wine – anything from boar to Toulouse sausage. It's ripe, vanilla-tinged, dry yet full, nicely textured, warmly tannin-undertoned and very friendly. Better than many Riojas.

SPANISH WINE　　WHITE

Marques de Riscal Sauvignon 1998　　14　C

Great with oysters.

**Nekeas Barrel Fermented Chardonnay
1997** `15.5` `C`

Chewy, woody, rich yet has delicate touches of soft fruit. An impressive concentration of flavours here.

USA WINE   RED

Fetzer Bonterra Cabernet 1995 (organic) `15` `E`

Fetzer Private Collection Cabernet 1994 `13.5` `G`

If it was six quid, instead of fifteen, it would be worth more points. A £15 wine must have some great presence and potency to justify its price.

Saintsbury Garnet Pinot Noir 1997 `13.5` `E`

Seven Peaks Cabernet 1996 `13` `E`

Thornhill Pinot Noir NV `13` `C`

USA WINE   WHITE

Bonterra Viognier 1996 (organic) `15` `E`

The '97 will be coming in soon (not tasted at time of going to press).

Fetzer Bonterra Chardonnay 1996 `14.5` `E`

Fetzer Private Collection Chardonnay 1996   `13.5` `F`

Bit much for my blood and my pocket. My palate enjoyed the texture and weight of fruit but didn't entirely feel comfortable with the 'look-at-me-aren't-I-a-clever-boy' flamboyance.

Seven Peaks Chardonnay 1997   `13.5` `E`

Thornhill Chardonnay NV   `15.5` `C`

FORTIFIED WINE

Stanton & Killeen Liqueur Muscat (half bottle)   `16.5` `D`

Creamy toffees, brandy butter, chocolate ice cream – is that enough of a mouthful? To be drunk with rich desserts.

SPARKLING WINE/CHAMPAGNE

Champagne Brossault Brut NV   `12` `G`

Champagne Brossault Brut Rose NV   `13` `F`

Chateau de Boursault Champagne Brut   `13.5` `G`

Joseph Perrier Champagne 1990   `12` `H`

Wouldn't put twenty-five quid on this nose, I must say.

Joseph Perrier Champagne NV

Lindauer Special Reserve NV (New Zealand)

Has more cheek than your average champagne.

Moet's Shadow Creek Blanc de Noirs (USA)

Moscato d'Asti Araldica 1997

Sweet apples, dry pears – plus bubbles – this is a hugely amusing aperitif.

Pelorus 1994 (New Zealand)

Curious ripe richness makes this vintage less classically dry and witty as it has been in the past.

Prosecco Vini dei Poeti 1997 (Italy)

Dry, classy, polished – many a champagne should be this accomplished.

Seaview Pinot Noir/Chardonnay 1994 (Australia)

One of Australia's strongest and tastiest challenges to Rheim's hegemony.

Veuve Clicquot Rich Reserve 1991 `13` `H`

Very rich and deep. Needs smoked or curried fish.

MAJESTIC

Majestic vastly extended its horizons this year. Last November, *Off-Licence News* reported that Majestic was to offer free case delivery anywhere in the mainland UK. Previously delivery had been limited to a 30-mile radius of each individual store. Majestic is now in a position to make such an offer because it has far wider national coverage than a few years back. The chain hit the 80-store mark early this year, with the opening of a store in Exeter and five more were scheduled to open in the financial year.

Expanding its home delivery service has been a high priority for Majestic. In January, it announced that it was to spend more on marketing the service with the aim of boosting home delivery sales to 30% of the company's total business. At the beginning of the year, about 5% of Majestic's sales came from home delivery. Around 200,000 copies of the company's catalogue are being mailed to customers or distributed through the stores. The move seems to be a response to the launch of the Wine Rack catalogue by the giant market leader, First Quench (the umbrella corporate name for the merged goliath of Victoria Wine and all Thresher's satellites). Mail order has always been a minor yet popular means of buying wine and with growing interest in home/internet shopping it is no surprise to see wine retailers investing in this area. Indeed, analysts believe wine will be one of the most dynamic areas of the home shopping market. (Didn't Nostradamus predict this four hundred years ago?)

Majestic is of course known as the wine-by-the-case retailer but this is no longer quite true with the opening of its new store at the ridiculously overhyped and utterly redundant £17 million Vinopolis wine Disneyland which opened in London in the summer of 1999. This store is Majestic's first to be licensed to trade as a normal off-licence, selling wines by the bottle rather than insisting on a minimum order of one case. Majestic expects the 5,000 sq ft store, one of the largest in the chain, to sell around 500,000 bottles a year with an annual turnover of around £2 million. While most of the customers are expected to be Vinopolis visitors, the store does have separate public access.

New store openings have been coming thick and fast at Majestic in recent years and the expansion looks set to continue. When announcing its interim results late last year, the retailer said it had identified some 60 locations where new outlets could be opened in the future. The company also said that on average consumers spent just over £5 on every bottle of wine purchased at Majestic – higher than the average spend at supermarkets.

More insight into the Majestic consumer was provided by a profile published in *Checkout* magazine. According to *Checkout*, Majestic caters for the serious wine consumer. The typical customer is a professional man who spends £100 per visit. *Checkout* looked at the Majestic's Southampton store where it found that at least six bottles were available for tasting at any one time and every month the store runs a themed tasting weekend organised by head office. Any doubts about the effectiveness of wine tastings as a marketing tool can be dispelled by the Southampton branch manager who says that these weekends can boost the sales of the featured wines by up to 600%.

From any point of view, Majestic has always been lean enough to be seen by wine buyers as a local entity, yet large and aspiring enough to have real purchasing muscle. It champions decent German wines, has a rich range of bubblies, good French ranges, and the new world is fully represented. If I were not a wine critic and thus ethically unable to buy shares in wine retailers, I would have unhesitatingly purchased Majestic shares, had I the money, when they became a plc. And I say this in spite of the odd *Guardian* reader who writes to me enraged that he can't buy a single bottle of the high-rating Majestic wine I have written about in my Saturday *Guardian* column but can only buy it as a component of a mixed case or as a whole case. One reader was so irritated he invited me to consider dropping Majestic from my purview. As is patently clear, I have absolutely no intention of doing any such thing.

Majestic Wine Warehouses
Odhams Trading Estate
St Albans Road
Watford WD2 5RE
Tel: 01923 816999
Fax: 01923 819105

SEE STOP PRESS SECTION AT END OF BOOK FOR LAST-MINUTE ADDITIONS OR UPDATES TO THIS RETAILER'S RANGE.

ARGENTINIAN WINE   RED

Marques de Grinon Diminio de Agrelo
Malbec 1997   `15.5` `D`

Lovely squashed fruit of richness with polished tannins.

AUSTRALIAN WINE   RED

Angove's Classic Red 1998   `15.5` `C`

Terrific savoury buzz about this wine. It has warmth, richness,
dryness, a great price ticket, and a strong finish of Marmite
and plums.

Angove's Classic Reserve Shiraz 1997   `14` `D`

Ripe, dry and very plummy on the finish. Hint of spice is nice.

Angove's Reserve Cabernet Sauvignon
1997   `16` `D`

Combines serious cabernet vegetality (admittedly subtle) with
ripe dry fruit of energy and eagerness-to-please.

Brian Barry Juds Hill Vineyard Merlot 1994   `13` `F`

Like a sweet sauce for roast duck.

Capel Vale Howecroft Cabernet Sauvignon
Merlot 1995   `12` `G`

Finishes a bit feebly for this sort of money.

Ironstone Shiraz Grenache, Margaret River and Swan Valley 1996 `16.5` `D`

Takes shiraz into a new dimension of such balance of fruit, acid and tannin, all so deftly interwoven and gorgeously textured, that it makes offerings from other Oz regions seem either mean or too expensive. It's a terrific wine with a hint of wildness.

Ironstone Vineyards Shiraz 1996 `13.5` `D`

Bit too juicy on the finish.

Mamre Brook Cabernet Shiraz 1996 `15` `D`

Resounds with richness, spiciness and dry yet full-throated fruitiness. Has a most attractive rustic undertone which gives it character.

Noble Road Shiraz Bin 1264 1997 `13.5` `D`

A sweet dark wine of interest to anyone with a mess of Italian sub-continental vegetables on their plate.

Penfolds Bin 35 Cabernet Sauvignon/ Shiraz/Ruby Cabernet 1997 `14` `D`

Juicy and well-meaning.

AUSTRALIAN WINE WHITE

Angove's Classic Reserve Chardonnay 1997 `15.5` `C`

Angove's Classic White 1998

Utterly scrumptious! The best Aussie white under £3.50 in the country. It has plumpness, richness and ripeness, but a serious edge of smoky melon. The potency and style of this wine are remarkable for the money.

Angove's Lock 5 Chardonnay 1998

Astonishing value. Has richness, vegetality, vibrancy and texture, and a rolling, lingering finish of understated ripeness. Remarkable chardonnay under £3.50.

Capel Vale Verdelho 1998

Unusually rich and gently spicy – great for oriental food. Very classy.

Ironstone Semillon/Chardonnay, Margaret River 1997

Lindemans Bin 65 Chardonnay 1998

A hugely elegant vintage, this, for a classic Aussie chardonnay. It has purpose, stealth, wit and warmth, and invites comparison with chardonnays daring to cost a lot more.

Mamre Brook Chardonnay 1997

Rich and energetic with a good flourish on the finish.

Mountadam Chardonnay 1997

Superb buttery, gently toasted aroma. Elegantly bodied full fruit, softly vegetal and ripe. Good array of mature fruit flavours and a rich nuts 'n' melon finish. Scrumptious! An exceptionally couth Aussie chardonnay.

Noble Road Verdelho Bin No 1356 1998

Curious ripe greengage edge. Has some hint of smoke, too. Perhaps a touch pricey but good with food.

Penfolds Koonunga Hill Semillon Sauvignon 1997

Superb texture, richness and ripeness. Outstanding vintage.

Wynns Coonawarra Riesling 1997

Stunning classic style of riesling with forward lemon fruit plus a hint of paraffin. A superb thirst-and-thought quenching wine.

Yenda Chardonnay 1998

Yenda Semillon Chardonnay 1998

CHILEAN WINE RED

Luis Felipe Edwards Pupilla Cabernet Sauvignon 1998

One of Chile's most claret-like cabs with its tannins and tenacity. The fruit is savoury, bold, textured and never too ripe. The finish is stylish and assured.

Santa Rita Reserva Cabernet Sauvignon, Maipo 1996

Hints of the cigar box Uncle Egbert's had since 1914, but the finish of the fat fruit is not so battle-scarred – it's all rich, soft fruit of great depth and savour.

Tocornal Vino Tinto NV   `13` `B`

Vistasur Cabernet Sauvignon 1998   `15.5` `C`

Bit sulphurous on the nose, the bottle I tried, so shake the bottle up, decant it and aerate its rich, dark, purple-prosed fruit.

CHILEAN WINE   WHITE

Luis Felipe Edwards Chardonnay 1998   `14` `C`

Not as exciting as previous vintages. The finish appears muted to me. Will it develop over 1998 and into '99? Who will give it a chance to? It'll be drunk young, alas.

Santa Rita Dona Paula Cabernet Sauvignon Rosé 1998   `14` `C`

Dry yet sunny and full of plummy freshness.

Tocornal Chilean White NV   `13.5` `B`

Vistasur Sauvignon Blanc 1998   `15.5` `C`

Deliciously restrained richness and well knitted fruit and acid. The balance is good – it leans towards texture and richness but never overstates its case.

ENGLISH WINE   WHITE

Pilton Dry Reserve 1996   `13` `B`

Has something to say for itself with fish and chips.

FRENCH WINE   RED

Beaune 1er Cru Les Chouacheux 1997   13 G

Beaune-Epenotes 1979   10 H

Did it climb this hill it's over? Has some sweaty aroma from the effort – but forty quid? Absurd.

Bourgeuil La Vernelle 1997   16 C

The essence of young great cab franc: cherry and raspberry, slate tiles, rich and ready. Very dry.

Bourgogne Rouge, Leroy 1996   13 F

Bouton d'Or Cairanne, Cotes du Rhone Villages 1995   16 C

Delicious baked, savoury fruit with a touch of dried fruit earthiness on the finish.

Brouilly Manoir du Pave 1998   11 D

Chateau de Bosc Cotes du Rhone 1997   11 D

Almost feeble compared to other Majestic reds less pricey.

Chateau de Candale, Haut Medoc 1996   14 F

Chateau Guiot Costieres de Nimes 1998   16.5 C

Wonderful tobacco-scented, herby richness. Blackcurrant, plums and a vegetal hint, lush yet firm tannins and a warm finish. Fantastic value.

Chateau Haut Mazieres, Bordeaux 1996   `12.5` `D`

**Chateauneuf-du-Pape, Domaine des
Senechaux 1996**   `14` `E`

Chenas Domaine des Pins 1998   `14` `D`

Has some individuality and potency. Possesses character and textured fruit to back it up.

Chinon les Garous, Couly-Dutheil 1997   `15` `D`

Claret Cuvee 090 1998   `14` `C`

No, don't laugh. It has some nice tannins and polite fruit. Bargain claret of meatiness and style. Very dry.

Claret Lot 278, Bordeaux 1997   `15` `C`

Corbieres Domaine Madelon 1998   `16.5` `C`

Magnificent bargain. Huge construct of ripe, deeply textured fruit of polish yet punch. Combines herbs and earth, hedgerow fruit, velvet and corduroy texture and a savoury finish. Remarkable for the money.

Corton Grancey Grand Cru 1995   `12.5` `H`

**Coteaux de Tricastin Domaine Saint
Remy 1997**   `15` `C`

The tannins are a varnish to the gentle earthiness of the soft fruit which is not remotely cloddish or rustic. Has real charm and drinkability.

**Coteaux du Tricastin, Domaine du Vieux
Micoulier 1995**   `14.5` `D`

Bit stern-visaged but not too bellicose on the finish where the dry earthiness melds well with the bramble fruit. A solid wine of some aplomb.

Cotes du Rhone Les Chevaliers aux Lys d'Or 1997

Intensely earthy and dry-cherry fruited.

Domaine Bois du Garn Grenache Syrah, Cotes du Vivarais 1996

Domaine de l'Ile St-Pierre Cabernet Franc 1998

More tannins here than your average racing saddle. As such it might seem fearsome but the fruit is also racy and urgent and the overall effect is of a quirky claret from a brilliant, undiscovered chateau. A great grilled food wine: savoury and cheroot-tinged.

Domaine de la Closerie St Nicholas de Bourgueil 1997 13 D

Domaine de la Janasse VdP de la Principaute d'Orange 1997 15 D

Spiced blackberries and a hint of dark cherry – loads of mature and controlled tannins (the wine will develop well if cellared for four or five years) and the whole effect is warm, spicy and rich.

Domaine de Rodes Grenache VdP d'Oc 1998 13 C

Interesting earthy structure.

Fixin Jaffelin 1996 12 E

Seems a tenner stretches the credulity more than the fruit stretches the palate.

Grenache/Cabernet VdP de l'Ardeche 1997   `16` `B`

What magnificent value here! Has hints of the peppery cabernet to match the juiciness of the grenache and the result is an excitingly underpriced plonk of rare quaffability and style.

La Fauve Merlot VdP d'Oc 1998   `15` `C`

Very soft leather here and it's very comfortable to sit in.

La Fauve Syrah VdP d'Oc 1998   `15.5` `C`

Brilliant drinking. Has class and quality fruit, a hint of spice, rich flavours of the warm south, and stylish tannins. A dry wine of versatile food-matching possibilities.

Macon St Gengoux 1997   `14` `C`

Interesting wine at this price, to try chilled with fish or, unchilled, with a blue mood. It tries very hard to raise the spirits and the texture and vegetal fruit is good.

Mas des Bressades Cabernet Syrah VdP du Gard 1996   `15` `D`

Delicious mature specimen where the rampancy of the earthy tannins has been tamed by the virile fruit and what we get is smooth richness and ripe pertinacity of purpose.

Morgon Jean Descombes 1998   `13` `E`

Some cries of protest from the tannins, subsumed with juicy gamay gushiness. Almost works, but at £7.50 I demand total efficiency.

Pernand-Vergelesses Jaffelin 1996   `12.5` `E`

Juicy, hint of dryness, severe price tag, not a severe enough level of complexity on the finish to rate higher.

Pinot Noir Cave de Ribeauville 1997   `14` `D`

Try it chilled with salmon. It's a partnership made not on earth.

Regnie Domaine Vallieres 1997   `15` `C`

Syrah VdP d'Oc 1997   `12` `B`

Syrah VdP du Cave Tain l'Hermitage 1998   `13` `C`

Bit juicy on the finish.

Vacqueyras Cave Co-op Beaumes de Venise 1997   `15.5` `C`

Never quite achieves its threatened earthiness but this is great for it's far from run of the mill. A mouth-fillingly rich, soft, luscious wine of deftness and dryness.

Wild Pig Red VdP d'Oc 1997   `16` `B`

Brilliant glugging value! Soft, ripe, it assuages the day's devilments and drearinesses. Has the plummy pertness to accompany chillied tomato soup (*my* recipe!).

FRENCH WINE   WHITE

Bourgogne Blanc, Leroy 1996   `10` `F`

Bourgogne Chardonnay Meilleurs Climats, Emile Trapet 1997   `14` `C`

Cante Cigale Rose de Saignee, VdP de l'Herault 1997   `14` `C`

Chablis, Caves les Viticulteurs de Chablis 1996 `15.5` `D`

Chablis Domaine Vocoret 1998 `13.5` `E`

If it was a fiver, I'd rate it higher for it has some soft yet steely charm. But at eight quid it isn't a firecracker and though far from a damp squib I would like more perfume and finish for my money.

Chardonnay Cuvee Australienne, VdP du Jardin de la France 1997 `13.5` `C`

Chardonnay Jean de Balmont, VdP du Jardin de la France 1997 `14` `B`

Chassagne-Montrachet Fontaine-Gagnard 1er Cru La Maltroie 1997 `10` `H`

Oh, come on!

Chateau du Sours Rosé 1998 `13` `D`

A dry, elegant rosé for Chelsea cocktail parties under large tents.

Chateau Haut Mazieres Blanc, Bordeaux 1996 `12` `D`

Oddly unfriendly and cold shouldering.

Chateau Meaume Bordeaux Rosé 1998 `13` `D`

Chenin Blanc VdP du Jardin de la France, Remy Pannier NV `14.5` `B`

Chinon Rosé Couly-Dutheil 1998 `13` `D`

Condrieu Guigal 1997

Rich baked sesame-seed aroma and high class. But the finish is a bit spiteful. A seventeen quid wine? If you like curate's eggs, yes.

Corton-Charlemagne, Bonneau du Martray 1996

Fifty quid? Something wrong somewhere.

Domaine de Raissac Viognier, VdP d'Oc 1998

I've bought two cases for the missus already. The remainder I'll leave for you. (She loves viognier so don't buy too much.)

Domaine de Saline Corsican Chardonnay, VdP de l'Ile de Beaute 1998

Nothing remotely saline about this – just clean, rich, uncluttered fruit.

Domaine des Fontanelles Sauvignon Blanc 1998

Utterly delicious ripe fruit, soft on the outside, crisp in the middle. Has elegance, bite, charm and real style.

Gewurztraminer Materne, Haegelin 1997

Unusually New World-ish gewurz in its richness, fatness, spicy butteriness and fullness.

Gewurztraminer Paul Zinck 1998

I'd be inclined to cellar it for three or four years and wait, chrysalis-like, for a 17-point wine to emerge.

Grand Ardeche Chardonnay 1997   `13.5` `D`

Some woody elegance and richness creeping into this vintage, but I find Latour's pretentions and pricing hard to swallow.

La Fauve Chasan 1998   `14.5` `C`

Delicious wine for food and/or mood. Rich, deep, smooth, multifaceted, this is bargain plonking. Great with grilled fish.

La Fauve Marsanne VdP d'Oc 1998   `13.5` `C`

Very rich and dry/fruity. Great with mackerel straight off the grill.

La Fauve Rosé de Syrah 1998   `14` `C`

La Ramillade Cotes du Rhone 1998   `15` `D`

A brilliantly dry wine for trout and all river fish. It has wonderful restrained herbiness and earthiness, yet it's never coarse, if coy.

Les Grands Clochers Chardonnay VdP d'Oc 1998   `13.5` `D`

Almost very good, then it goes a bit squashy and bruised-fruity on the finish.

Les Grands Vignes Cotes du Rhone Cairanne 1997   `11` `C`

Montagny 1er Cru, Chateau du Cray 1997   `12` `E`

Moulin Touchais, Coteaux du Layon 1986   `16.5` `E`

Gorgeous toasted honey fruit with nuts and sesame seeds.

Muscadet Cuvee du Homard 1998   `14` `B`

Cheap and good for lobster, too. Is Muscadet back to form?

Muscadet sur Lie Chateau de Goulaine 1997

`12.5` `C`

Ah! Muscadet! Wherefore art thou?

Muscadet sur Lie Chateau la Touche 1998

`13.5` `C`

An unusually rich and ripe Muscadet.

Muscadet sur Lie Grand Mouton, Louis Metaireau 1996

`11` `D`

Muscat Riquewihr, Bott-Geyl 1997

`14` `E`

Very delicate and nervous. Lot of money for a bag of nerves but it's impressively sniffable and slurpable – its finesse will be fatally bruised by robust food.

Organic Sauvignon de Touraine Domaine des Maisons Brulees 1998

`14` `C`

Competent rather than exciting, it does have some texture on the finish. But a fiver? Bit over the top.

Pinot Blanc Haegelin d'Alsace 1997

`15.5` `D`

Wonderful spicy food wine. Great gobbets of rich melon fruit, suggestion of raspberry and gooseberry, and a ripe finish.

Reuilly Beurdin 1998

`12` `D`

Bit of a young tart.

Riesling Bollenberg, Haegelin 1997

`16` `D`

For riesling lovers this presents a dilemma: do I sip it now, getting plenty of air in with each slurp to aerate the minerals and fruits,

or do I lay it down for five or six years (or more) and let these
flavours become more bewitching, concentrated, curious?

Riesling Grafenreben, Bott-Geyl 1996 `14` `E`

**Sancerre 'Clos du Roy', Paul Millerioux
1998** `13.5` `E`

Bit pricey compared with other Majestic sauvignons which are
more suave.

Sauvignon de Touraine Joel Delaunay 1998 `14.5` `C`

Nice bit of herbaceousness to the rich fruit which has texture and
some degree of tension. It is better than many Sancerres.

Sauvignon Lot 279, Bordeaux 1998 `13` `C`

Bit dull on the finish. Worthy starter, though.

St Veran Les Deux Moulins 1997 `12.5` `D`

Sylvaner, Paul Zinck 1998 `12.5` `C`

Tokay Pinot Gris Ribeauville 1997 `15.5` `D`

Tokay Pinot Gris, Haegelin d'Alsace 1997 `16` `D`

A spicy, peachy, soft yet dry, creamily-edged TPG with loads of
flavour and depth. A wine for oriental food.

**Vivian Ducourneau VdP des Cotes de
Gascogne 1998** `16` `C`

Wonderful cheeky fruit: refreshing, bold, pineappley and rich yet
riddled with great acids so the overall effect is elegant, nutty and
very charming.

Vouvray Tris de Nobles Grain, Domaine Bourillon Dorleans 1995 (50cl) `16` `F`

Beautiful richness and ripeness. Put it down for a few years and it'll be even more complex.

GERMAN WINE   WHITE

Grans Fassians Riesling, Mosel 1997 `13` `D`

Oberemmeler Rosenberg Riesling Kabinett Halbtrocken 1993 `14` `C`

Serriger Heiligenborn Riesling Spatlese 1990 `15.5` `C`

Still young, still developing petrol. Great honey and acids. Needs five or six more years.

ITALIAN WINE   RED

Amarone della Valpolicella, Tedeschi 1993 `14` `E`

Cavalchina Bardolino 1997 `15` `C`

Centine Toscanna, Banfi 1997 `16` `D`

Utterly compellingly quaffable richness and controlled jamminess. Has loads of freshness, good scaffolded tannins, and a richly applied outer coat of savoury fruit.

Chianti Remole Frescobaldi 1997 `14` `D`

Col di Sasso Sangiovese & Cabernet 1997 `15` `C`

Very dry finish but loads of fruit upfront, ripe and savoury and rather bold.

Cortenova Merlot, Grave del Friuli, Pasqua 1997 `13` `B`

Dogajolo Toscano Carpineto 1997 `14` `D`

Juicier than previous vintages, this ornately labelled wine is extremely keen to delight.

Montepulciano d'Abruzzo Barone Cornacchia 1997 `15.5` `C`

Brilliant ripeness and richness here: savoury, deep yet utterly quaffable.

Nipozzano Riserva Chianti Rufina Frescobaldi 1996 `14` `E`

Juicy ripeness on a level I've not before discovered from this estate. However, there is a straining after elegance. The fruit is gentled by its tannins rather than coarsened.

Primitivo del Salento 1997 `15.5` `C`

Superb plumpness and ripe richness here. Terrific texture and urgent-to-please fruit.

Recioto della Valpolicella Tedeschi 1995 (half bottle) `15.5` `D`

The sweetness is often offputting but this old warhorse of a wine is delicious with robust meat dishes and risottos, where the balsamic richness of the thick fruit is totally at home.

ITALIAN RED

Rosso di Sicilia 1997

Simple cherry-ripe earthiness.

Val del Trono Aglianico del Vulture 1996

Lot of loot, lot of wine. Has a hint of mineralised, volcanic acidity, a touch of licorice to the spiced plum and leather blackcurrants, and a lovely tannically interwoven structure. A splendid wine of texture and tension.

Valpolicella Classico, Santepietre 1997

ITALIAN WINE WHITE

Bianco di Sicilia, La Toricella 1997

Castello di Tassarolo, Gavi 1997

Cavalchina Bianco di Custoza 1997

A custardy Custoza! What a lovely tipple. Not blowsy or too creamy, no; the crisp appleskin acidity melds perfectly with the richer overtones to provide class, style and drinkability. A fish wine plus . . .

Chardonnay/Pinot Grigio Delle Venezie, Pasqua 1997

Frascati Superiore, Campoverdi 1997

Moscato d'Asti, Bava 1997

Soave Classico, Santepietre 1997 14 C

NEW ZEALAND WINE WHITE

Marlborough Gold Chardonnay 1998 13 D

Curious sour finish.

Marlborough Gold Sauvignon Blanc 1998 14 D

Good acidic finishing power from a suggestion of fatness as it starts work.

Nautilus Chardonnay, Marlborough 1995 15.5 E

Oyster Bay Chardonnay, Marlborough 1997 14 D

PORTUGUESE WINE RED

Duas Quintas Tinto, Douro 1995 16 D

Makes a great change from cabernet or merlot. A beautifully polished wine, fleshy yet smooth, rich yet not overblown, it finishes with individuality and precision. Great price for such quality.

SOUTH AFRICAN WINE RED

Drostdy-Hof Merlot 1996 13.5 D

SOUTH AFRICAN WINE   WHITE

De Wetshof Estate 'Lesca' Chardonnay 1997   `14` `D`

Franschoek Barrel Fermented Chenin Blanc 1997   `15.5` `C`

Swartland Steen 1998   `12` `B`

I find the aroma of muscle cream a touch unfriendly.

SPANISH WINE   RED

Artadi Vinas de Gain Rioja Crianza 1996   `14.5` `E`

Not your usual vanilla-edged Rioja, this is more strict with itself and is dry, deep and herby.

Berberana Dragon Tempranillo 1997   `14.5` `C`

Dry yet juicy, charred yet fleshy. Great little mouthful.

Costers del Gravet, Celler de Capcanes 1997   `16` `E`

Most surprising muscle yet litheness here. It begins with such delicacy and restrained fruit, then strikes hard and rich and full of style and flavour as it reaches the throat. A terrific balance of fruit/acid/tannins.

Marques de Grinon Rioja 1997   `15` `D`

Very ripe and forward. Great for food.

Marques de la Musa Tempranillo Conca de Barbera 1997 — 13 | B

Marques de Murietta Rioja Reserva 1995 — 14 | E

Perfectly mature, very ripe Rioja which needs matching food – manchego cheese soufflé with anchovy sauce poured over is my choice.

Mas Collet Tarragona 1997 — 16.5 | D

Gorgeously alive and vibrant with a lovely hedgerow sweetness of soft fruit, and dry, twiggy tannins in great harmony. Superb stuff!

Muga Rioja Reserva 1995 — 12 | E

Tempranillo Vina Armantes Calatayud 1997 — 15.5 | C

Savoury, dry, full (never, though, blowsy or too ripe), deeply flavoured and finishes with some multi-layered richness of fruit.

Vina Ardanza Rioja Reserva, La Rioja Alta 1990 — 14 | F

A special occasion treat with its dry woodiness and rich tannins.

SPANISH WINE — WHITE

Marques de la Musa, Viura Chardonnay 1997 — 13 | B

Bit appley and simplistic.

SPANISH WHITE

Martin Codax Albarino Rias Baixas 1997 `14.5` `D`

Bit pricey for such patent individuality.

Muga Rioja 1998 `10` `D`

Pretty ugly.

Vinas del Vero Barrel Fermented Chardonnay, Somontano 1996 `15` `D`

USA WINE RED

Beringer Appellation Zinfandel 1996 `14` `E`

Lot of money for a dry Rhone style Zin but it does possess heft and hauteur if it isn't as exuberant or as spicy as zin can be. It has a three-piece suited, tightly woven seriousness about it.

Beringer Harmonie Pinot Noir/Gamay 1996 `13.5` `D`

Gallo Sonoma Barelli Creek Merlot 1995 `15` `F`

Very sweet fruited yet dry tannined. The leatheriness is subtle, the fruit bold.

Gallo Sonoma Frei Ranch Zinfandel 1995 `14` `F`

Juicy, dark, ripe, with soft tannins giving out to dryness on the texture of the fruit. Is this wine already too old? Not as exciting as eighteen months ago, that's for sure.

Ironstone Vineyards Cabernet Franc 1996 `15.5` `D`

Fleshy yet firm, controlled yet full of wise old franc fruit.

Ironstone Vineyards Merlot 1997

Very jammy and textured but has lovely tannins which make for a balanced mouthful of ripeness, not too dry or over-fruity, and a lingering finish.

Prosperity Red NV

The label is worth the price of admission and what you get is dry, savoury fruit of pizzazz and purpose. Huge serious fun quaffing.

USA WINE
WHITE

Beringer Appellation Fume Blanc 1997

A wonderfully woody, elegant yet ripe wine of great depth of flavour and layers of insistent deliciousness. A wine of scrumptious drinkability.

Beringer Californian Sauvignon Blanc 1997

Unlike other sauvignons this one is rampant and richly textured, not dry nor caring to be, and yet it finishes with dry-seeming fruit of great style.

Beringer Californian Zinfandel Blush 1998

Repulsive mush. It is a sin to turn zin into fruit juice.

Calera Chardonnay, Central Coast 1996

Intense, concentrated, very rich, beautifully textured, slightly grassy and sensual (even a touch feral), and superbly well kitted out to handle food – like a roast farmyard fowl.

Fetzer Viognier 1998 `16.5` `E`

Lovely limpid, lush, lively – a wine of ineffable finesse yet apricot-scented and fruited richness. A rare treat. Fruit to read by, think by, listen by.

Ironstone Vineyards Gold Canyon Chardonnay 1997 `15.5` `D`

A rich, almost spicy chardonnay made of well-baked but not over-roasted fruit with pert and pertinent acids. A bargain for such Californian elegance at this price.

Prosperity White NV `15` `C`

Super-charged simplicity yet depth here – lots of ripe melon with perfect hand-in-hand help from pineapple acidity. Great with fish and Mr Fish.

FORTIFIED WINE

Amontillado Seco Napoleon, Hidalgo `16` `E`

Pour it over ice cream or simply use a spoon to lap it up. It's molasses-rich but not sweet. Wonderful treat for the in-laws.

Pedro Ximenez Viejo Napoleon, Hidalgo `15` `E`

Usual biting, acerbic, sour performance. The best pick-me-up of an early evening for crusty old farts and their brethren.

Taylor's Quinta de Terra Feita 1986 `17` `G`

Like taking a draught of liquidised hedgerow plus sun, an allotment of herbs and even a hint of very soft, beautifully developed tannins. The texture is balsamic and gripping, the effect is heady, the residual memory is of doing something rather naughty.

SPARKLING WINE/CHAMPAGNE

Ayala Champagne NV `12` `G`

Ayala Champagne Rosé NV `11` `G`

Bollinger Grande Annee 1990 `11` `H`

Bouvet Ladubay Saumur NV (France) `14.5` `E`

Cava Verano, Freixenet NV `15.5` `C`

Conde de Caralt Cava Brut NV `16.5` `D`

As elegant a cava as they come. Knocks a thousand Champagnes into oblivion.

**De Telmont Grande Reserve
Champagne NV** `13.5` `G`

Hunter's Miru Miru 1996 (New Zealand) `15` `F`

More elegant than a thousand Champagnes. More gentility in the fruit department, more style in the acid.

Jacquart Brut Mosaique Champagne NV `12` `G`

Jacquart Vintage Champagne 1990 `13` `H`

Too expensive by half.

Louis Roderer Quartet NV (California) | 14 | | G |

Moet's Shadow Creek Blanc de Noirs (USA) | 14 | | E |

Oeil de Perdrix Tradition NV | 14 | | G |

Taittinger Champagne Brut NV | 12 | | H |

The price is, frankly, difficult to swallow when many cavas, at a quarter of the price, are no less charming.

Taittinger Comtes de Champagne 1990 | 10 | | H |

Seriously overpriced at £75.

Yellowglen Pinot Noir Chardonnay NV (Australia) | 13.5 | | E |

ODDBINS

Fame is a fifteen minute commodity nowadays yet even with such ephemeral celebrity comes the penalties of fame. Oddbins' buying and marketing director, Mr Steve Daniel, was doubtless chuffed when Oddbins was the subject of a TV documentary in late 1998 only to find that as well as offering due praise the programme took a few swipes too. In being ambushed by a TV documentary Oddbins is in good company. The Royal Opera House and St Paul's Cathedral – not to mention that horrendous golf club in north London which confirmed that the pastime (it is hardly a sport) attracts psychopathic Neanderthals and other assorted chauvinists – have both invited the cameras in to find that the end-result did not exactly accentuate the positive. In her series, Vintners Tales on BBC2 (which I have never seen but readers who have caught it are unanimous in praise of its restful qualities), Ms Jancis Robinson said, I believe, that she found Oddbins to be a treasure trove of offbeat bargain bottles but she also said that the shops' scruffy, underpaid and over-educated sales staff treated her like absolute dirt. Ms Robinson also suggested that Oddbins gives preferential treatment to brands owned by its parent company, Seagram.

In his defence, Mr Daniel explained, so I was further told, that the company did not have a dress code for its employees. He also somewhat curiously (but superbly) found himself describing his own staff as misfits. What is more the spellchecker on my computer seems to concur. It does not recognise the word Oddbins but suggests oddballs instead. Mr Daniel did not exactly deny that they were badly paid, saying that few people in the wine industry were paid particularly well. With regard to Seagram, he said that the Seagram brands it carried would have to sell or there would be no point in having them in the store. Besides it is a bit naive to imagine that Seagram would not receive special treatment from its own wine store – which it bought in the first place to ensure U.K. distribution of its brands denied shelf-space (or certainly hampered in this ambition) by the activities of Britain's well-entrenched brewery-owned wine chains. From Seagram's point of view, there would be no point whatsoever in owning a bunch of wine shops which observers more qualified than I claim to be one of the less profitable areas of the corporation's business. My only comment on this is that I wish the BBC had asked Mr Giles MacDonagh of the *Financial Times* to conduct an interview with Mr Daniel and then we might have got a real fight on our hands. There was a marvellous spat between these two when Mr MacDonagh, who possesses the sharpest mind on the *FT*'s food and drink writing team, was rude about Oddbins in an article and Mr Daniel vigorously protested. However, Mr MacDonagh does not own a TV nor does he possess any ambition to appear on it. He is, however, a compelling reason to read the pink 'un on a Saturday; though I say this knowing him purely as an acquaintance I find more entertaining than anyone else writing on wine or, his other bowstring, German history. He is more gossipy than a fishwife, more withering than Jeremy Paxman.

It is the accusations about staff rudeness which are the most interesting because it is something I have heard before. People tend to say that Oddbins staff are the most knowledgeable of all the off-licence chains and can be among the most helpful, but there is always the odd observation about shop staff being offhand or coming over as smart Alecs. Youth is surely a factor in this alleged arrogance; twenty years ago I found myself getting unusually heated with one hormonally precocious chap who insisted I was wrong about a Loire grape variety when I had no wish to dispute his muddleheadedness but simply buy a bottle of wine and escape. It has been suggested to me that the fact of staff being over-educated graduates but underpaid serfs has something to do with this attitude. It seems a pointless debate to me since I do not admit of the existence of the concept of over-education, only the reverse. It has also been suggested that Oddbins bullies wine suppliers into giving lower prices. What a laughable idea. If there is bullying it is the mildest name-calling in comparison with the systematic pressure applied by the large supermarkets. It's nothing more than haggling for the prices the retailer considers the customers will consider reasonable. If this gets bargains for Oddbins' customers and readers of this book, who are we to complain?

Interestingly, in the same issue of *Off-Licence News* which carried this story, the weekly newspaper also reported that Oddbins had been named Wine Merchant of the Year in the International Wine Challenge* for the ninth time in 11 years, though the weekly journal surprisingly made no attempt to combine the stories, even running them on separate pages. This seems to neatly encapsulate the ambiguity or contradiction of Oddbins' critics. The vast majority of Oddbins' customers, I am quite sure, do not find the staff anything but charming and as far as I am aware actually warm to the so-called 'unconventional' approach because it reflects the way most shops are run and staffed nowadays. At least Oddbins' employees don't chew gum; not on duty at any rate.

While his TV career may not progress further, Mr Daniel has had a busy year overseeing a number of interesting developments at Oddbins. Late last year, the company opened two more Ultimate Wine Stores, one in the City of London and one in

---

* A pompous and magnificently overhyped event where retailers and wine producers part with money to have their wines, thousands of them, tasted by groups of so-called experts who, in one anecdote I heard from a one-time judge, can be anyone from a young Oddbins employee to a struggling wine writer. For a couple of years, I was invited to be a judge on one of the umpteen tasting panels but I have always declined on the grounds that it is of no benefit to my readers or my schedule. The work is unpaid though the organisers make a decent profit and hand out piles of certificates. The wine trade, especially wine suppliers, think it wonderful. I regard the whole thing as fatuous theatre.

Reading. The company now has four of these larger outlets, which can carry the entire Oddbins' range of 1,200 wines, and more are planned. In addition to carrying the full Oddbins arsenal, these shops have areas which can offer wine tastings throughout the day, parking facilities, a larger cigar Humidor carrying 50 different cigars and a separate fine wine section offering 300 to 400 additional wines from smaller parcels. Such an establishment, with its faint atmosphere of louche disorder, is simply a cleverly interior-designed consumer temple aimed at the deeper-pocketed male worshipper.

Oddbins is also expanding its international horizons. The retailer now has four stores in Dublin and attracted considerable attention in February when it acquired a 1,000 sq ft in Calais originally operated by Victoria Wine. The shop is situated in the Cite Europe shopping centre, where Tesco also has an outlet, and will aim to capitalise on returning UK boozers keen to take advantage of France's lower alcohol duties. Oddbins says: 'The flow of customers across the Channel does not seem to be subsiding and if current trends continue and government taxing does not change, the flow will increase. The store in Calais will carry the same range as the shops in the UK and customers can even ring ahead and have an order ready for collection.' Smart thinking; it leaves more time for customers to enjoy a blowout French lunch.

Oddbins also relaunched its mail order service last year and is currently in the process of developing a web site. The site at www.oddbins.co.uk was launched just before Christmas 1998 but more pages are being designed. The full site was due to be launched later in 1999. In fact, in February 1999, the preliminary Oddbins website was asking for feedback from shoppers about what kind of site they would like to see, offering a prize of a case of Billecart-Salmon Champagne for the best suggestion. Oddbins, when it comes to ideas like this, is ahead of all other high street wine shops.

Oddbins
31-32 Weir Road
Wimbledon
London SW19 8UG
Tel: 0181 944 4400
Fax: 0181 944 4411

**SEE STOP PRESS SECTION AT END OF BOOK FOR
LAST-MINUTE ADDITIONS OR UPDATES TO THIS
RETAILER'S RANGE.**

ARGENTINIAN WINE

Balbi Cabernet Sauvignon, Mendoza 1997   `15.5` `C`

Nutty blackcurrant and plum, a hint of spice and a touch of tannin.

Balbi Malbec, Mendoza 1997   `13` `C`

Balbi Malbec Shiraz, Mendoza 1997   `16` `C`

Great fruit as warm and soft as an old teddy bear. Really nuzzles up to the taste buds.

Balbi Shiraz, Mendoza 1997   `16` `C`

Real Aussie shocker here: spicier, more concentrated, richer and more excitingly textured than an Oz likely lad for the same money.

Isla Negra Bonarda, Mendoza 1997   `15` `C`

Isla Negra Malbec, Mendoza 1997   `15` `D`

Isla Negra Syrah, Mendoza 1997   `16.5` `D`

More rampant than any Aussie for the same money. Terrific style here.

Las Lilas Malbec Sangiovese, Mendoza 1997   `15.5` `C`

Brilliant value dry glugging and food friendly fruit here.

ARGENTINIAN RED

Marques de Grinon Dom Agrelo Malbec, Mendoza 1996

`16` `D`

A very stylish malbec. Has perfume, presence, persistence, loads of flavour, dryness and depth, and a finish of considerable finesse yet weight.

Marques de Grinon Duarte Malbec, Mendoza 1996

`15` `C`

Norton Reserve Cabernet Sauvignon, Mendoza 1997

`15.5` `D`

Norton Reserve Malbec, Mendoza 1997

`16` `D`

Great complexity of tonal fruit flavours here. Textured, ripe, untroubled, calm, very classy.

Norton Reserve Syrah Cabernet, Mendoza 1997

`15.5` `D`

Norton Salmon Label Cabernet Sauvignon, Mendoza 1995

`14` `D`

Good scrap between the fruit and the tannins.

Norton Salmon Label Malbec, Mendoza 1995

`14` `D`

Juicy and super-ripe but the tannins swing it in the end.

Norton Salmon Label Merlot, Mendoza 1995

`15` `D`

Juicy but has an aggressive undertone of spice and savouriness.

Valentin Bianchi Cabernet Sauvignon, San Rafael 1996

Very posh, potent and beautifully polished. Speaks with a very elegant plum in its mouth.

Valentin Bianchi Malbec Reserve, San Rafael 1996

Savoury richness with a hint of creme fraiche.

Valentin Bianchi Malbec, San Rafael 1996

AUSTRALIAN WINE RED

Annie's Lane Cabernet Merlot 1996

Annie's Lane Cabernet Merlot, Clare Valley 1997

Annie's Lane Shiraz, Clare Valley 1997

Campbells Robbie Burns Shiraz, Rutherglen 1997

Balsamic textured and fruit-tinged. Warms the cockles.

Chateau Reynella Basket-Pressed Shiraz 1995

Wonderfully rich beast of racehorse litheness with cart-horse endurance and muscle. It is highly aromatic, maturely fruity, deeply complex as it crushes all resistance from the taste buds, and the finish makes a much vaunted northern Rhone syrah seem positively jejune and spineless.

**Cranswick Estate John's Vineyard
Grenache, Riverina 1996** 13 D

**Cranswick Estate Nine Pines Vineyard
Cabernet Merlot, Riverina 1996** 13.5 D

---

d'Arenberg Red Ochre, McLaren Vale 1997 14 C

Juicy but well developed and dry.

**d'Arenberg The Custodian Grenache,
McLaren Vale 1996** 15 E

Yep, Indian cooks could build dishes round it.

**d'Arenberg The Footbolt Old Vine Shiraz,
McLaren Vale** 15.5 D

I'd have to demand an Indian vegetarian feast to enjoy this rich, palate-pounding wine. Has a black belt in tongue twisting.

**d'Arenberg The High Trellis Cabernet
Sauvignon, McLaren Vale 1997** 15 D

Even tastes a bit high. But this is not a criticism. Drink it with rare grouse or pheasant.

**d'Arenberg The Ironstone Pressings
Grenache Shiraz. McLaren Vale 1996** 14 F

The essence of Aussie refined fruit juice. The tannins are tame but decisive.

d'Arry's Original Shiraz Grenache, McLaren Vale 1997   16 D

Rampant fruit which takes no prisoners. Lovely stuff to match against an old style coq au vin.

Deakin Estate Cabernet Sauvignon, Victoria 1998   13 C

Deakin Estate Shiraz, Victoria 1998   13.5 C

Elderton Cabernet Sauvignon, Barossa 1996   16 F

Has a handsome gamut of flavours running from dry and savoury to rich and sweet. Fine Wine Stores.

Elderton Merlot, Barossa 1996   14 G

Fine Wine Stores.

Elderton Shiraz, Barossa 1996   17 F

Hums and literally vibrates with spicy, savoury fruit of massive depth. Fine Wine Stores.

Elderton Tantalus Shiraz/Cabernet Sauvignon 1997   14 D

Rather refined and cucumber-sandwichish for an Aussie.

Hillstowe Udy's Mill Pinot Noir, Lenswood 1997   14 E

Well, well – reminds me of my youthful indiscretions with Clos de Tart.

Merrill's Mount Hurtle Bush Vine Grenache, McLaren Vale 1996 `13.5` `D`

Mount Helen Cabernet Sauvignon Merlot 1996 `13.5` `E`

Mount Ida Shiraz 1996 `14` `E`

Nepenthe Vineyards Lenswood Pinot Noir 1997 `13` `F`

Fine Wine Stores.

Normans Lone Gum Shiraz/Cabernet Sauvignon 1997 `12` `C`

Normans White Label Cabernet Sauvignon, South Eastern Australia 1998 `13` `D`

Normans White Label Merlot, South Australia 1998 `13` `D`

Penny's Hill Shiraz, McLaren Vale 1996 `11` `E`

Fine Wine Stores.

Seppelt Terrain Series Cabernet Sauvignon 1996 `14` `D`

Tatachilla Cabernet Sauvignon, McLaren Vale and Langhorne Creek 1996 `14` `E`

Perfectly mature and ripely ready for the parched throat.

**Tatachilla Clarendon Vineyard Merlot,
South Australia 1997** `16` `F`

Very big wine with towering level of developed fruit and lovely
tannins. Zipping excitement.

Tatachilla Shiraz, South Australia 1998 `15.5` `D`

Resounds in layers of spice, soft plums and berries, lovely warm
subtle tannins and a great wallop on the finish.

Wakefield Shiraz, Clare Valley 1997 `15` `D`

It's the richness of the texture! Wonderful!

**Wirra Wirra Church Block Cabernet Shiraz
Merlot 1997** `15.5` `E`

Incredibly smooth and well polished. So elegant!

**Wirra Wirra Original Blend Grenache
Shiraz, McLaren Vale 1997** `16.5` `E`

Lovely lingering depths of cigar-tinged fruit. Also has some
catering chocolate and some superb layers of berries and solid
tannins. Exceptional wine.

**Wirra Wirra Vineyards The Angelus
Cabernet Sauvignon 1996** `13` `F`

Fine Wine Stores.

**Wynn's Coonawarra Estate Cabernet
Shiraz Merlot 1996** `14` `E`

Hint of spice, lots of ripe tannins, fruit well held within. Classy
and rich.

Yarra Valley Hills Cabernet Sauvignon 1996

Yarra Valley Hills Warranwood Pinot Noir 1998

Tobacco juice.

AUSTRALIAN WINE WHITE

Annie's Lane Riesling, Clare Valley 1998

A wine to quaff now or to lay down for three or four years to get more concentrated flavours and integration.

Bethany Riesling, Barossa 1997

Campbells Liqueur Muscat, Rutherglen NV (half bottle)

A magnificent Christmas pudding wine of great depth. Has baked fruit and molasses, toffees and toasted nuts. Incredibly good value for money. A real ambrosia of a wine.

Cranswick Estate Barrel Fermented Semillon, Riverina 1997

A real Thai fish dish wine. Has terrific complex acids.

Cranswick Estate Zirilli Vineyard Botrytis Semillon, Riverina 1996

Medicinal, thick, rich, very sweet but with the textured fruit so well served by the brilliant tannins.

---

d'Arenberg The Olive Grove Chardonnay, McLaren Vale 1998 `14.5` `D`

Most unAustralian in its dry richness and acidic style. Must be the olives.

---

d'Arenberg White Ochre, McLaren Vale 1998 `14` `C`

Very perfumed and ornate.

James Halliday Botrytis Semillon 1996 (half bottle) `16.5` `D`

Superb waxy sweet fruit with thrilling toffee-nosed rotten grapes giving it breadth, depth and luxuriousness.

Knappstein Riesling, Clare Valley 1998 `16` `D`

Love its bravura, richness and insouciant sense of style! Yes, it's ripe but it still, being riesling, achieves elegance.

Lindemans Bin 65 Chardonnay 1998 `16` `C`

Supremely sure of itself, this well-established brand showing, in its '98 manifestation, what a great year this is for Aussie whites from the region (Hunter Valley). This has great hints of warm fruit balanced by complex crispness and acidity. A lovely under-a-fiver bobby dazzler.

Mount Helen Chardonnay, Central Victoria 1997 `16.5` `E`

Utterly compelling in its woody vegetality, hay and melon and a finish of beautifully reserved, slightly smoky richness. Better than a thousand white burgundies.

113

Nepenthe Vineyards Lenswood Sauvignon Blanc 1998 `15` `E`

Interesting bruised fruit edge, elegant and biting, to some highly individual flavours.

Penfolds Trial Bin Adelaide Hills Chardonnay 1996 `14.5` `F`

Expensive powerhouse which needs posh food and thin flickering candles. A wine to give a Jewish princess to wash her feet in.

Penny's Hill Chardonnay, McLaren Vale 1997 `16` `E`

Individualistic, incisive, interesting and richly food friendly.

Peter Lehmann Semillon 1998 `14` `D`

Needs time to settle down and find the right partner. Shall we say six months? And risotto with squid ink?

Pewsey Vale Riesling, Eden Valley 1997 `15` `D`

Rothbury Estate Hunter Valley Verdelho 1998 `15.5` `D`

Something different, spicy and plump and food friendly, to purge the blues at the end of the day. A florid wine, fit for choosy throats.

Seaview Chardonnay, McLaren Vale 1997 `15.5` `C`

Loaded with frolicsome fruit, piled high with flavour.

Tatachilla Sauvignon Semillon, McLaren Vale & Adelaide Hills 1998 `15.5` `D`

Delicious marriage of perfect partners: dry, lovely rich yet calm fruit and a decisive finish. (Oh dear, that makes it sound more like a divorce.)

Wakefield Riesling, Clare Valley 1998   13   D

One to keep down for two years or so. Will be terrific.

**Wirra Wirra Scrubby Rise Semillon/
Sauvignon/Chardonnay, McLaren Vale &
Adelaide Hills 1998**   14.5   E

Engaging medley of fruits here. Dry and charmingly assembled.

**Yalumba Watervale Riesling, Clare
Valley 1997**   13   D

Needs a year more.

**Yarra Valley Hills Kiah Yallambee
Chardonnay 1998**   12.5   E

Bit sloppy on the finish for nine quid.

CHILEAN WINE   RED

**Carmen Reserve Cabernet Sauvignon,
Maipo 1996**   15.5   D

**Carmen Reserve Grande Vidure Cabernet,
Maipo 1997**   16   D

Very Bordeaux-like in its dry tannins. But the blackcurrant fruit comes zinging through.

Carmen Reserve Syrah, Maipo 1997

Carta Vieja Cabernet Sauvignon, Maule 1997

Casablanca Santa Isabel Estate Cabernet Sauvignon 1997

Has such dry depth but, paradoxically, with such weepiness of cassis-edged fruit that the drinker is deliciously puzzled. Ravishing now, I rather fancy it will over eighteen months develop coffee and tobacco manners.

Cono Sur Pinot Noir 1998

Very rich and ripe, not classic, but feral raspberries and truffles are detectable and the texture is superdeep. But it elevates itself over ten thousand red burgundies asking five times more.

Domus Aurea Cabernet Sauvignon, Macul 1996

Plenty of pretension here from the label to what sticks in the throat.

Isla Negra Cabernet Sauvignon, Rapel 1998   15.5   C

A deliciously hedgerow-fruity wine of charm and rich, unmannered unpretentiousness.

La Palmeria Cabernet Sauvignon 1998   15.5   C

Gorgeous, gorgeous, gorgeous.

La Palmeria Merlot, Rapel 1998   16.5   C

It combines that wonderful Chilean double-whammy of food fitness and great, concentrated, complex drinking. Gorgeous stuff.

La Palmeria Reserve Cabernet Sauvignon/Merlot 1998
17 **D**

So accomplished and unshowy yet demonstratively brilliant, textured, balanced, very smooth and hugely drinkable. It literally purrs with stylishness.

Luis Felipe Edwards Pupilla Cabernet Sauvignon 1998
16 **C**

One of Chile's most claret-like cabs with its tannins and tenacity. The fruit is savoury, bold, textured and never too ripe. The finish is stylish and assured.

Morande Aventura Carignan 1997
13.5 **C**

Morande Aventura Cesar 1997
13 **C**

Morande Aventura Cinsault 1997
13.5 **C**

Morande Aventura Malbec 1997
13 **C**

Porta Limited Edition Cabernet Sauvignon, Cachapoal 1998
16.5 **C**

An affront to deep-seated cabernet values, this compelling wine: serious yet jammy, dry yet spicy and warm, fruity and with drawn out complex depths.

Santa Carolina Red, Maule 1998
15.5 **B**

Brilliantly fruity yet classy red.

Santa Rita Medalla Real Special Reserve Cabernet Sauvignon 1997
16 **E**

Has a cough mixture echo as it descends but this fits the rest of the picture here which is of a restless, rich, spoiled, arrogant wine of total wicked charm.

Santa Rita Reserve Merlot Unfiltered, 1996 `16` `D`

Compelling richness and texture, classy fruit, longevity of finish and delicious, serious balance of elements.

Veramonte Cabernet Sauvignon, Alto de Casablanca 1997 `15` `D`

Vinified from old cheroots and well-ripened plums and blackcurrants.

Veramonte Merlot, Alto de Casablanca 1997 `14.5` `D`

Vina Porta Cabernet Sauvignon, Maipo 1998 `15` `C`

Delicious tea/cocoa/tobacco and cherries/plums/blackberries. Complex? Nope. Just ridiculously delicious.

Vina Porta Reserva Unfiltered Cabernet Sauvignon 1995 `17` `E`

Utterly stunningly savoury cabernet with tannins, tenacity and sublime typicity.

CHILEAN WINE   WHITE

Carmen Chardonnay, Central Valley 1998 `17` `C`

Goes through the classy gamut from perfume, big tongue-lashing smoky fruit, to a layer of fruits as it descends. Remarkably complete wine for a fiver.

Carta Vieja Chardonnay, Maule 1998 `13.5` `C`

Carta Vieja Sauvignon Blanc, Maule 1998 `15.5` `C`

Brilliant sharp fruit here – pinpoint sharp, not tart – with lovely freshness and lemonic incisiveness.

**Casa Lapostolle Cuvee Alexandre
Chardonnay 1997**   `E`

One of Chile's greatest chardonnays. Has superb balance (richness, ripeness, length of flavour) and it's so classy it hurts.

Casa Lapostolle Sauvignon Blanc 1998 `16` `D`

Superb nutty richness, elegance and a biting, lingering finish. A truly great s.b. for the money.

**Casablanca Neblus Botrytis Chardonnay
1997 (half bottle)**   `C`

Odd, very odd, a dry honey wine of nuttiness and waxy texture but not a hint of sweetness. Fine Wine Stores.

**Casablanca Santa Isabel Gewurztraminer
1998** `13` `D`

Huge crushed rose petal aroma but the fruit is raw and unknitted. Needs eighteen months.

**Casablanca Sauvignon Blanc, Casablanca
1998** `15.5` `C`

Incisive, interesting, elastic-fruited, and delicious on the untenanted tongue or one lined with dead mollusc shreds.

Domus Proa Chardonnay 1997 `13.5` `D`

Very plump and rather fleshy on the finish. Delicate it ain't.

CHILEAN WHITE

Errazuriz Chardonnay Reserva, Casablanca 1997

Deep and richly resounding, it has hauteur and highly developed manners. Very classy and cool.

Errazuriz La Escultura Estate Chardonnay, Casablanca 1998

Nuts, touch of smoke, hint of spice, complex soft and hard fruits, lingering finish of polish and satin-textured excitement. A lovely wine.

Errazuriz Wild Ferment Chardonnay, Casablanca 1998

Seems a touch confused on the finish but this may be folie de jeunesse. I'd be inclined to age it for at least eighteen months; a minor miracle might emerge.

La Palmeria Chardonnay 1998

Restrained, rich, charming acidity, subtle lemon/lemon flavours.

Santa Carolina Chilean Sauvignon 1998

Fantastic smoked salmon wine for Christmas. Crisp and grassy with a lovely hint of rich vegetal plumpness – but always dry and wise.

Santa Rita '120' Rosé Cabernet Sauvignon 1998

Easily the most delicious rosé I've tasted since sharing a bottle staring into Melanie Bach's eyes in 1966.

Veramonte Chardonnay, Alto de Casablanca 1998

14 D

Oddbins seems to go for blatant fruit in their chardonnays from Chile.

Vina Porta Chardonnay, Cachapoal 1998

14 C

Curiously fat and fulsome chardonnay, brimful of flavour. Not subtle, this wine.

FRENCH WINE RED

Baron Saint-Pierre, Coteaux du Languedoc 1998

14.5 B

Very plump and soft with nary a scary tannin in sight (though they do lurk).

Chateau de Combebelle Saint-Chinian (Comte Cathare) 1997 (bio-dynamic)

15.5 D

Lovely sweet edge to very cigar-edged fruit and soft, ripe tannins. Superb quality fruit.

Chateau de Fesles Anjou Rouge Vieilles Vignes 1997

17 D

Quite magnificent cherry/raspberry/plum fruit with softly chewy tannins and a hint of almond and licorice. A subtle assembly of complex comforts.

Chateau de Passedieu, Cotes de Bourg 1996

14 C

Chateau Depaule, Cabardes 1998

Tobacco, coffee, plums – plus texture and tension between fruit and acidity. Complex and bold.

Chateau Maris Minervois (Comte Cathare) 1996 (bio-dynamic)

Ruffled velvet, unruffled fruit, warm tannins – the sheer texture of the thing is exciting enough.

Chateau Paveil de Luze, Margaux 1996

Shows a biting turn of pace. Great tannins. Needs two or three years more.

Chateau St Jean de Conques, Saint Chinian 1998

Ripe and dry.

Cotes du Rhone Les Arbousiers, Remejeanne 1997

Good comforting level of controlled earthiness and dry plummy fruit.

Cotes du Rhone Les Genevriers, Remejeanne 1997

Much like the Les Arbousier, really. Touch drier and friskier, maybe.

Crozes Hermitage Les Pierrelles, Belle 1996

Crozes Hermitage Meysonniers, Chapoutier 1996

Cuvee de Grignon Rouge, VdP de l'Aude 1998
15 B

What charm and highly drinkable earthy fruit here. Terrific stuff.

Domaine Remaury Cabernet Sauvignon VdP d'Oc 1998
17 C

Wonderfully invigorated, soulful, charcoal-chewy fruit of immense depth and richness. The price is absurd given the potency and flavour on offer here.

Domaine Saint Jullien Coteaux du Languedoc 1998
15.5 C

Superb brightness, ripeness, texture and fullness of flavour here. Lovely tannins.

Domaines des Aires Hautes Malbec, VdP d'Oc 1998
15.5 D

Wonderful, chewy, savoury tannins and huge depth of fruity richness.

Givry 1er Cru Les Grandes Berges, Tatraux 1997
12 E

Mas Saint-Vincent Coteaux du Languedoc 1998
16.5 C

A stunningly complete and captivatingly rich masterwork of herbs, earth, hedgerows and passion.

Metairie du Bois Syrah, VdP d'Oc 1998
16 C

Brilliant subtle spicy fruit, dry-edged and darkly fulfilling. Terrific value for money.

Ptomaine de Blageurs Syrah, VdP d'Oc 1996 `14` `C`

Ptomaine de Blageurs Vin de Table 1996 `13` `C`

St Joseph Le Grand Pompee, Paul Jaboulet Aine 1996 `13` `E`

Stowells of Chelsea Vin de Pays du Gard (3-litre box) `13.5` `B`

Price band is the equivalent for 75cl.

FRENCH WINE   WHITE

Bourgogne Blanc Cuvee Saint Vincent, Girardin 1997 `12` `E`

Chateau de Fesles Rosé d'Anjou 1998 `13.5` `C`

Touch sweet.

Chateau de la Genaiserie Coteaux du Layon, Yves Soulez 1997 `16` `E`

A wonderful spicy gooseberry and honey fruit crumble wine which is never too sweet or too obvious. It will repay laying down for five or six years.

Cuvee de Grignon, VdP de l'Aude 1998 `13` `B`

Basic, tart, tongue-tingling. Good for fish barbecues.

Domaine Cady Coteaux du Layon St-Aubin 'Harmonie' 1998 (50cl)   17   E

Utterly gorgeous sweet wine with hints of candied peel, apple, creme brulee and ripe butterscotch. Has a finish of Greek thyme honey.

Domaine de Fontbonne Sauvignon, VdP d'Oc 1998   14.5   C

Hint of fatness and curiously dry ripeness. Tasty and good with complex shellfish preparations.

Domaine Ournac Viognier, VdP d'Oc 1997   13   C

Hautes Cotes de Nuits Blanc, Jayer Gilles 1996   14   G

Rather tired, old-hat but definitely white Burgundian, overpriced, run-down opulence. Fine Wine shops.

James Herrick Chardonnay 1997   15   C

One of southern France's most accomplished, classically styled, bargain chardonnays.

Macon Davaye Domaine des Deux Roches 1998   15.5   D

Always an excellent white burgundy, this vintage has outstanding balance and crispness.

Macon Villages Tete de Cuvee, Verget 1997   14.5   E

Has some real elegance and gentle vegetal bite.

FRENCH WHITE

**Menetou-Salon Morogues 'Clos de Ratier',
Pelle 1998**　　13　E

**Metairie du Bois Sauvignon Blanc, VdP
d'Oc 1998**　　15.5　C

Excellent sauvignon fruit – squashed gooseberry and bright acidity. Dry, great with fish.

**Metairie du Bois Syrah Rosé VdP
d'Oc 1998**　　15　C

Terrific quality fruit for the money. Textured and taut, cherryish and charming.

**Montagny 1er Cru, Domaine Maurice
Bertrand 1997**　　13　E

Pouilly-Fume Domaine Leburn 1998　　13.5　E

Extremely, lushly lemony.

**Pouilly-Fume Le Champ des Vignes,
Tabordet 1998**　　12　E

**Saint-Aubin 1er en Remilly, Domaine du
Chateau de Puligny-Montrachet 1997**　　13.5　G

Delicious but worth fourteen quid? No but it has some good smoky richness, delicate acidity and a pleasing finish in a New World mould.

**Saint-Romain, Domaine du Chateau de
Puligny-Montrachet 1997**　　12　F

Drinkable but not deft enough to rate higher.

Sancerre Domaine de la Rossignole 1998　　12.5　E

Sauvignon 'Le Lac', VdP du Jardin de la France NV `13` `B`

Energetic and eager – rather basic but it has some merit matched with food.

Savennieres, Chateau de Varenne 1997 `13` `E`

Rather floridly acidic and austere.

St Veran Les Chailloux, Domaine des Deux Roches 1998 `14` `E`

Chardonnay in a minor key, true. But then after the Rachmaninov of some New World chardonnays, this Schubert impromptu will come as a charming surprise.

St Veran les Cras, Lassarat 1996 `12` `G`

Fine Wine shops.

Stowells of Chelsea Vin de Pays du Tarn (3-litre box) `14` `B`

Price band is the equivalent for 75cl.

Vouvray Moelleux Les Girardieres 1ere Trie 1996 `15` `G`

GERMAN WINE

WHITE

Durkheimer Fronhof Scheurebe Trockenbeerenauslese, Kurt Darting 1998 (50cl) `15.5` `G`

Immensely sweet with barely an echo of the grapefruit style the scheurebe grape is famous for. But lay it down – six or seven years or more – and a 20-point masterpiece will emerge.

Kunstler Riesling Kabinett Halbtrocken, Rheingau 1997

`14` `D`

Interesting aperitif. Or great with smoked fish.

Messmer Burrweiler Altenforst Scheurebe Spatlese, Pfalz 1997

`14` `E`

Different, the scheurebe grape. Said to taste of grapefruit. Over the next two or three years, so will this specimen.

Messmer Burrweiler Schlossgarten Riesling Kabinett Halbtrocken 1997

`13` `D`

Messmer Riesling, Pfalz 1997

`13` `C`

Basic, if improving.

Munsterer Kapellenberg Riesling Kabinett Kruger-Rumpf 1997

`13` `D`

I daresay given seven or eight years this might put on four points. Or it might not.

Ruppertsberger Reiterpfad Scheurebe Beerenauslese, von Buhl 1994 (half bottle)

`17` `H`

Astonishing richness and honeyed grapefruity lushness give it an unusual multi-layered, dry effect in what is a sweet wine. It will age for twenty years, but you can enjoy it now with fruit tarts.

Schultz-Werner Gaubischhofheimer Herrenberg Riesling Kabinett, Rheinhessen 1997

`14`

Von Buhl 'Armand' Riesling Kabinett, Pfalz 1997   `15` `E`

Classic riesling with that hint of dry honey and mineralised richness. Will develop typical petrol undertones over the next ten years.

Von Buhl Forster Riesling Spatlese, Pfalz 1997   `16` `E`

Gorgeous amalgam of texture, tautness, fruit/acid harmony of overall sheer deep class. Highly drinkable now but cellared it will improve, mature, develop and become concentrated and complex (ten years or more).

Westhofener Westhofner Kirchspiel Scheurebe Kabinett, Wittman, Rheinhessen 1997   `14` `D`

GREEK WINE   RED

Boutari Agioritiko, Nemea 1994   `15.5` `E`

Domaine Constantin Lazaridi Amethystos Cava 1995   `14` `G`

Sweet chocolate and ripe tannins. Fine Wine Stores only.

Gaia Estate Agiorgitiko, Nemea 1997   `14` `E`

Expensive curiosity. Heaps of tannins.

Gaia Notios Red, Peloponnese 1998   `14` `D`

Interesting chocolate edge to the wine, dry and very different.

Gerovassiliou Red, Epanomi 1996   15.5   E

Dry but full of cherry ripe fruit of assertive personality. Yoghurt on the finish.

Kosta Lazarides Amethystos Cava, Drama 1995   13   G

Subtle it isn't. Nor's the price tag.

Ktima Kosta Lazaridis Amethystos Red, Drama 1997   13.5   E

Drying out on the finish.

Ktima Kyr-Yianni Ramnista, Naoussa 1997   16   D

Totally out of order: a Greek with muscles like a midi red, tannins like a very pricey Barolo and a finish which recalls a great Crozes-Hermitage. Yet for all these metaphors it writes in its own style.

Ktima Kyr-Yianni Syrah, Imathia 1997   18   E

A monumental syrah of such stunning herby richness and power it has few equals either in the Rhone or in the Antipodes. The layers of fruit peel off in delicious tannic frenzy and the finish is like being kissed by a hallucinating angel.

Ktima Kyr-Yianni Yianakahori, Imathia 1997   15.5   E

Immensely chunky and rippling, well-muscled tannins and ripe fruit.

Ktima Voyatsi 1997   16   E

Astonishingly savoury tannins and chewy texture. Deep, black fruit of style and richness.

Mavrodaphne of Patras NV (50 cl) `15.5` `D`

**Spiropoulos Porfyros, Pelponnese 1997
(organic)** `14` `D`

Very dry and rustic.

Strofilia Red, Anavissos 1995 `15` `D`

Lovely warm undertone to some crisp, clean fruit. Makes a great
change from chardonnay. Very ripe but has some gorgeous rich
tannins to balance it all out.

Tsantali Syrah, Halkidiki 1996 `13` `D`

Bit too lush and ripe for me.

**Tselepos Cabernet Sauvignon,
Peloponnese 1996** `15.5` `E`

Deliciously alert and warmly tannic cabernet of some weight
and class.

GREEK WINE   WHITE

Antonopoulos Adoli Ghis 1997 `13.5` `D`

Bit flat on the finish.

Antonopoulos Mantinia 1997 `14.5` `C`

Lemon hints to some fleshy fruit.

Boutari Visanto, Santorini 1993 (50cl)

Unusual pudding wine with hints of nuts, honey, melon. Yet, curiously, it finishes like dry apple skin.

Gaia Notios White, Peloponnese 1998

Lovely lilting flavour of under-ripe ogen melon on the finish. There is also a hint of raspberry. An individual quaffer of great charm.

Gaia Thalassitis, Santorini 1998

Has some interesting deep minerals. A wine from Atlantis? Quite likely.

Gentilini Robola 1997

Gerovassiliou Chardonnay 1996

The oddest chardonnay you'll ever taste. Rich roasted sesame seeds is the theme.

Gerovassiliou White, Epanomi 1998

Bit ragged here and there. It's the sort of wine which tastes wonderful in Skiathos but not in Skegness.

Kosta Lazaridis Amethystos Fume Blanc, Drama 1998

Old smoky cream finish of some charm rounds off some crisp clean fruit.

Kosta Lazaridis Amethystos Rosé, Drama 1998

One of the tastiest and dryest rosés I've tasted.

**Kosta Lazaridis Amethystos White,
Macedonia 1998**　`14.5`　`D`

Has some dry and steely class and the fruit, no slouch, haunts
the finish deliciously.

**Kosta Lazaridis Chateau Julia Assyrtiko,
Adriani 1998**　`13.5`　`D`

**Kosta Lazaridis Chateau Julia Barrel
Fermented Chardonnay, Adriani 1998**　`14`　`E`

Subdued, dry, nutty edge. Not typical chardonnay until the wine
has quit the throat for twenty seconds – a hint of burgundian
vegetality settles.

Spiropoulos White, Mantinia 1998 (organic)　`14`　`C`

Softly intentioned but the hint of crispness and vague cos lettuce
and gooseberry fruit is decisive.

Strofilia Nafsika, Anavissos 1997　`13.5`　`D`

Odd creamy fruit finish.

Strofilia White, Peloponnese 1997　`15`　`D`

Lovely warm undertone to some crisp, clean fruit. Makes a great
change from chardonnay.

ITALIAN WINE　RED

Barbaresco Chiarlo 1995　`13`　`G`

Bricco Zanone Barbera d'Asti 1995　`14`　`C`

Casa Girelli Teroldego Rotalianio 1997 | 13 | D |

Dolcetto d'Alba 'Rousori', Icardi 1998 | 16 | E |

The sweet raisiny edge like prunes and cream with cherries on top is trademark Dolcetto. This also has unusually exciting tannins.

Duca di Castelmonte Cent'are Rosso 1996 (Sicily) | 15 | C |

Felline 'Albarello' Rosso del Salento 1997 | 16 | E |

Dry yet rich and resoundingly full of soft fruit flavours. Immensely food-friendly.

Gagliardo Barbera d'Alba 1998 | 14 | E |

Sweet and sour fruit.

Icardi Barbera d'Asti 'Suri di Mu' 1997 | 15.5 | E |

Tremendously satiny texture. The fruit is lush yet dry, confident and all-embracing.

Masi Modello delle Venezie 1997 | 14 | C |

Dark cherry fruit and attendant brisk tannins. Solid glugging here.

Torre Vento Primitivo del Tarantino 1996 | 13.5 | C |

Tre Uve Ultima NV | 13 | D |

Trulli Negroamaro 1997 | 14.5 | C |

Warm, savoury, very polished and almost sedate in its mouthful, it packs a punch of gentility, yet style. Hint of leather to it.

Trulli Primitivo 1997

Spicy, warm, herbal, rich, yet has a stealth-of-foot deftness as it quits the throat. Generous quaffing here and food-friendliness.

ITALIAN WINE WHITE

Cantine Gemma Moscato, Piemonte 1997

One of the world's most charming, undiscovered aperitif wines. Sure, it's floral and petticoaty – but it's wonderful.

Gavi La Chiara 1997

Maculan Torcolato, Breganze 1997

Toffees and a light fruit crumble make up the sweet fruit. It needs to have three more years of bottle age – then, pow!!!

Trulli Chardonnay Salento 1998

Delicate progression of richness yet delicacy courses over the taste buds here, leaving one refreshed and panting for more. It would be easy to quaff this wine too quickly and miss its abundant charms as it trips, with variegated steps, down the throat.

Trulli Dry Muscat 1998

Lovely floral edge, dry as you like it, and not a sissy side in sight. A sophisticated aperitif or to go with minted fish dishes and tomato tarts.

NEW ZEALAND WINE RED

**McDonald Church Road Reserve Merlot,
Hawkes Bay 1996** `14` `F`

**Montana Fairhall Estate Cabernet
Sauvignon, Marlborough 1996** `13` `F`

**Montana Reserve Barrique Matured
Merlot, Marlborough 1996** `15.5` `E`

Improving very nicely in bottle – delicious ripeness, maturity
and richness. Pulls itself delicately back from OTTness.

**Villa Maria Cabernet Merlot, Hawkes
Bay 1996** `14` `E`

NEW ZEALAND WINE WHITE

**Montana Reserve Riesling, Awatere
Valley 1998** `13` `E`

Muted on the finish.

**Montana Reserve Sauvignon Blanc,
Marlborough 1998** `14` `E`

Deft interweaving of restrained fruit and mildly flirtatious
acidity.

Selaks Sauvignon Blanc 1996 `15.5` `D`

PORTUGUESE WINE   RED

Caves Alianca Palmela, Douro 1996   `15` `C`

Pegos Claros, Palmela 1994   `15.5` `E`

Perfectly mature and full of soft fruit and developed tannins.

Quinta da Lagoalva, Ribatejo 1995   `15` `D`

Very raisiny and full of dry spicy plum flavours. A real food
wine.

PORTUGUESE WINE   WHITE

Esporao Branco 1996   `12` `D`

SOUTH AFRICAN WINE   RED

Beyerskloof Pinotage, Stellenbosch 1998   `13.5` `D`

**Blaauwklippen Cabernet Sauvignon/Merlot
1996**   `13.5` `C`

Blaauwklippen Shiraz 1997   `13.5` `D`

Touch cosy-cosy for my palate but great with curries.

Boschkloof Cabernet Sauvignon 1997 `15.5` `D`

Tobacco, sweet fruit (plus spicy plums) of blackberries and some exotic vegetal entity, and solid tannins on the finish. Terrific food wine.

Boschkloof Reserve Cabernet Sauvignon/ Merlot 1997 `14` `E`

Can't quite see what makes it reserve, except the price. But it's game enough – and, indeed, up for game dishes.

Fairview Carignan, Coastal Region 1998 `13` `D`

Very juicy vintage for this estate, the '98.

Fairview Shiraz Mourvedre 1998 `17.5` `D`

The aroma is initially of fine Cuban cigars from tobacco grown on the plain overlooking the Baie de Cerdos. This finesse, powerfully augmented by the nigh 15% of alcohol as the ripe, spicy fruit floods the mouth, breaks up into a variety of soft fruits with light, soft tannins. A big yet lithe wine of rugged charms (yet smooth).

Fairview Zinfandel Carignan, Paarl 1998 `14.5` `D`

Greatly improved since I first tasted it, this is very soft and ripely assertive.

Fontein Cinsault Merlot, Paarl 1998 `12.5` `C`

Fontein Merlot, Paarl 1998 `14.5` `C`

Delightful leather softness, rich tannins and a plump finish.

Glen Carlou Les Trois 1996 `16` `D`

Lovely dryness and fruit here. Real thrill as the wine goes down. Terrific tannins. Fine Wine Stores.

Glen Carlou Pinot Noir 1998　　　13.5　E

The finish is a touch clodhopping but the initial fruit attack is
clods of fruit firmly stamping their feet.

Ken Forrester Grenache Syrah, Stellenbosch 1998　　14　D

Very soupy and rich.

Klein Constantia Shiraz 1997　　13.5　E

Tobacco scented, juicy, tannins on the finish squeeze out
the fruit.

Kumala Reserve Cabernet Sauvignon 1997　　17　E

Wonderful one-off marvel of sublime cabernet class: pepper,
cheroots, blackberries, tannins – it's got the lot. Plus superb
textured richness.

Longridge Bay View Cabernet Sauvignon 1998　　14　D

Juicy.

Longridge Bay View Merlot 1998　　14　D

Chewy and soft with a hint of sweet cherries on the finish.

Longridge Bay View Pinotage 1998　　15　D

Very free with its charms which run unchecked across the
taste buds.

Radford Dale Merlot, Stellenbosch 1998　　14　E

Very unusual merlot of morello cherries and dry tannins. The
texture is such that it claws at the throat.

SOUTH AFRICAN RED

Savanha Cabernet Sauvignon 1997   `15` `D`

Savanha Merlot 1997   `14` `D`

Savanha Shiraz, Western Cape 1997   `13` `D`

Slayley Shiraz Stellenbosch 1997   `14` `E`
Fine Wine Stores.

Stellenzicht Pinotage 1998   `17` `E`
Astonishingly richly textured, as clotted as a hawser, and it's difficult to unravel the fruit from the tannins. But the complexity
is considerable – it includes tobacco and chocolate – and the
finish manages, paradoxically, to achieve elegance in spite of the
dynamic, galloping fruit.

Stellenzicht Shiraz 1998   `15` `E`
Very sweet-edged fruit. A great Balti wine.

Veenwouden Merlot, Paarl 1996   `13` `F`

Von Ortloff Cabernet Merlot 1995   `13` `D`
Fine Wine Stores.

Von Ortloff Merlot 1997   `14` `D`
Fine Wine Stores.

SOUTH AFRICAN WINE   WHITE

Boschkloof Chardonnay Reserve 1997   `13` `D`
A little flatulent rather than dynamic. Fine Wine Stores only.

Collingbourne Cape White NV 14 B

Danie de Wet Chardonnay sur Lie,
Robertson 1998 15 C

An individual bottling exclusive to Oddbins and though delicate
and richly restrained, it has some quiet class.

De Wetshof Bon Vallon Chardonnay 1998 13.5 D

Eikendal Chardonnay, Stellenbosch 1998 14 E

Touch smug on the finish, but then it's so healthy and full
of itself!

Fair Valley Bush Vine Chenin Blanc,
Coastal Region 1999 15.5 C

Beautifully perfumed, crisp and with lingering pear and melon
fruitiness.

Fairview Cyril Back Semillon, Paarl 1998 16 D

Hugely lingering yoghurt/raspberry/melon/lime fruit. Quite
delicious. The delicacy of the impact is impressive and very,
very classy.

Fontein Chardonnay, Worcester 1998 14 C

Creamy and very mouth-filling. Great with spiced mussels.

Fontein Colombard, Robertson 1998 12.5 C

Glen Carlou Chardonnay 1998 15.5 E

Lots of richness and roustabout fruitiness here yet it finally
comes clean and cool and finishes with some style.

Glen Carlou Reserve Chardonnay 1997

Fine Wine shops.

Ken Forrester Scholtzenhof Chenin Blanc, Stellenbosch 1998

Creamy, dusty edge of clashing interest. Has some tension and contrast.

Klein Constantia Chardonnay 1998

Warmth, wit, richness and layered flavours of fruit from wood, to melon, to lemon and spicy pineapple.

Klein Constantia Riesling 1998

Odd – needs Thai fishcakes to shape it up, ship it out and down the throat.

Klein Constantia Sauvignon Blanc 1998

So much better than almost any Sancerre! It's richer, more concentrated, better defined and more impactfully elegant.

Longridge Bay View Chardonnay, Western Cape 1998

Fat and a touch florid, but with fat fish it'll become more lithe and energised.

Longridge Chardonnay, Stellenbosch 1998

Seems rich and ripe enough – indeed it might be OTT to some palates – but the finish is less animated.

Mount Disa Sauvignon Blanc, Coastal Region 1998

Neethlingshof Gewurztraminer, Stellenbosch 1998

| 14 | D |

Interesting partner for moules marineres.

Radford Dale Chardonnay, Stellenbosch 1998

| 14 | E |

A food wine in that the richness is on the cloying side.

Scholtzenhof Petit Chenin, Stellenbosch 1999

| 15.5 | C |

Remarkable value for money here – a wine of dash, difference and a little daring. It's dry, refreshing and elegant.

Slayley Chardonnay 1997

| 15.5 | E |

Big smoky fruit, baked and not remotely bashful. Fine Wine shops.

Stellenzicht Chardonnay, Stellenbosch 1997

| 15 | D |

Lovely texture, ripeness and fullness of fruit but never overdone or too obvious.

Stellenzicht Sauvignon Blanc, Stellenbosch 1998

| 13.5 | D |

Dry and very drinkable but seven quid is stretching it as far as the fruit goes.

Stellenzicht Semillon Reserve, Stellenbosch 1998

| 15 | E |

Lot of loot (nigh on a tenner) but the wine is a superb amalgam of wood and warm, vegetal fruit.

Vergelegen Reserve Chardonnay 1997 `16.5` `E`

Always one of the Cape's most elegant chardonnays statements.
A magical Meursault-like wine!!

Vergelegen Sauvignon Blanc 1998 `15.5` `D`

Elegance and understatement.

Von Ortloff Chardonnay 1996 `16` `D`

Very delicate, deliberate, beautifully woody and classy wine. Fine
Wine shops.

SPANISH WINE   RED

Artadi Orobio Tempranillo, Rioja 1998 `15` `D`

Textured, taut, nicely glycerol-edged and soft.

Cosme Palacio y Hermanos, Rioja 1997 `15` `D`

A fully developed, dry, purposeful rioja of depth and style.

Enate Tempranillo Cabernet Crianza, Somontano 1995 `16.5` `D`

Gorgeous aromatic fruit of a lovely balance of elements offering
richness, texture and a great clinging finish. A classy wine of
great style.

Espiral Tempranillo Somontano 1997 `15` `C`

La Cata Tempranillo, La Mancha 1998 `14` `C`

Dry but fruity.

La Vicalanda de Vina Pomal Reserva, Rioja 1995

Too ripe on the finish for me (or for thirteen pounds).

Olivares Dulce Monastrell 1996

'Almost tastes like a dish in itself,' said Karen at Oddbins, and she's right. This is a stickily sweet red which will go with fruit cake, a hangover, a hospital cure for a blue mood, and it'll even waken the dead palate. It is never monodimensional and simply gooey – rather, it's textured, multi-layered and teasing. Great with blue cheese.

Piedemonte Merlot/Cabernet Sauvignon, Navarra 1998

Brisk non-nonsense blackberries and leathery softness.

Taja Gran Reserva, Jumilla 1994

What's it got that the Taja Tinto hasn't? More elegant tannins, deeper and more lingering textural qualities and staying power.

Taja Reserva, Jumilla 1994

Very accomplished depth of richness. Strains at raunchiness but achieves only polish and aplomb.

Taja Tinto, Jumilla 1998

Chocolate and dry cherries, raisins, and a hint of vegetality combine to make this richly textured wine totally ravishing.

Vina Sardana Tempranillo, Calatayud 1997

Unusual tempranillo, full of dry cherries, a hint of spice, and savoury damsons.

SPANISH WINE — WHITE

**Albacora Barrel Fermented Verdejo/
Chardonnay, Vino de Mesa 1996** `14` `D`

Burgans Albarino, Rias Baixas 1997 `13.5` `D`

Torres Vina Esmeralda, Penedes 1998 `15` `D`

A wonderfully fresh, lime-edged aperitif wine of considerable
style and wit. Less adolescent than previous vintages, the '98
has some real chutzpah.

USA WINE — RED

Bonny Doon Cardinal Zin 1997 `12.5` `E`

Silly posturing on behalf of the fruit.

Bonterra Zinfandel, Mendocino 1996 `16.5` `E`

A wonderfully exotic specimen of warmth and immediacy.
Spicy, chewy, softly tannic, hedgerow fruited, it has immense
charm and forwardness.

Canyon Road Cabernet Sauvignon 1998 `14` `D`

Sweet and soft and saved from OTTness by the developed
tannins.

Canyon Road Merlot, Geyserville 1997 `13.5` `D`

Lot of juice here.

Fetzer Syrah 1996   16   E

Lovely dry richness under which beats a wild, soft heart of characterfulness.

Fetzer Vineyards Home Ranch Zinfandel 1996   15.5   D

Lovely spicy fruit here. Dry yet full of flavour and textured ripeness.

Fetzer Vineyards Private Collection Merlot, Mendocino 1996   16   G

Rampantly dry/sweet fruit.

Fetzer Vineyards Private Collection Petite Sirah, Mendocino 1996   17.5   G

It operates like this: the tannins hold the rich, sweet, concentrated fruit like pearls of plush cassis on the taste buds for what seems like an age. A wonderful special occasion wine.

Franciscan Vineyards Pinot Noir 1997   13   E

J Lohr Paso Robles Syrah, California 1996   13   E

Fine Wine Stores.

Marietta Old Vine Red Lot 22, Geyserville NV   13   E

More Cal-juice.

Wing Canyon Cabernet Sauvignon 1994   13   G

Fine Wine Stores.

USA WINE WHITE

Ca'de Solo Bloody Good Pink 1997 `15` `D`

Ca'de Solo Bloody Good White 1997 `13` `D`

Canyon Road Chardonnay 1998 `14` `D`

Fat and forty-something.

Echo Ridge Fume Blanc 1996 `15.5` `C`

Fetzer Bonterra Chardonnay 1996 `16` `E`

Deliciously classy, rich, controlled and well balanced. A sane reason to spend eight quid on a wine.

Fetzer Private Collection Chardonnay 1997 `13.5` `F`

Bit much for my blood and my pocket. My palate enjoyed the texture and weight of fruit but didn't entirely feel comfortable with the 'look-at-me-aren't-I-a-clever-boy' flamboyance.

Fetzer Viognier 1998 `16.5` `E`

Lovely limpid, lush, lively – a wine of ineffable finesse yet apricot-scented and fruited richness. A rare treat. Fruit to read by, think by, listen by.

Landmark Overlook Chardonnay 1997 `13` `F`

A point for every pound it costs. Yes, it's got some woody charm to it but . . . but . . . but . . . At thirteen pounds, buts are not what you want.

Mariquita 1995

Brilliant value tippling. Bold and bonny – full of gluggable fruit.

Prodigy Chardonnay 1998

Hoof-thundering richness and creaminess here. Needs a dish of flash fried scallops.

Prodigy Grenache Rosé, California 1998

Wonderfully chewy and rich and the hint of trollop's cosmetic on the finish does nothing to mar the performance.

Three Valleys Late Harvest Muscat 1995

Brilliant dry/rich muscat fruit with a steel edge and a heart of spicy wit. Brilliant aperitif.

SPARKLING WINE/CHAMPAGNE

**Billecart-Salmon Cuvee Nicholas Francois
Billecart Brut 1991**

Very fine, very expensive, for the well-heeled tongue only.

Cuvee Napa by Mumm Blanc de Blancs NV

Utterly delicious near bone-dryness and classically styled echoic richness. Better than Mumm can make in France.

Deutz Marlborough Cuvee (New Zealand) 13.5 E

Has a faintly fleshy finish.

Graham Beck Blanc de Blancs (South Africa)

13 | E

Gratien & Meyer Saumur Cuvee Flamme Brut NV (France)

12 | E

Henri Harlin Brut NV

15 | G

Engagingly dry and delicate. An excellent brut style.

Lindauer Special Reserve Brut NV

14.5 | E

Has finesse and dryness. Class, too.

Mumm Cordon Rouge Cuvee Limitee 1990

13 | H

Too much money for the level of excitement on offer.

Pierre Gimonnet et Fils 'Cuis 1er Cru' Blanc de Blancs Brut NV

10 | G

Chardonnay all through, and as such some may find the finish too warm.

Seppelt Great Western Brut (Australia)

13.5 | D

Shadow Creek Californian Blanc de Noirs

14.5 | E

SPAR

In last year's guide I made reference to Spar UK managing director Mr Garry Craft and the bold plans he had for Spar to fight back against the supermarkets with top brands, better own labels, ready-to-eat hot food, in-store dry cleaning and 24-hour opening (their latest initiative, by the by, is in-store cashpoint machines). Spar is, I am glad to report, continuing the fight stoutly but it is doing so without Garry Craft who left the company only days after I penned his fighting words. Most interestingly, it was reported that Mr Craft was leaving his job to 'pursue other career options' and is looking to use his retail expertise within a multiple environment. In human resources doublespeak, does this not mean that he was looking for a job with a supermarket chain? Mr Craft's position incidentally was taken by a man called Morton Middleditch, a name worthy of Damon Runyon.

Mr Craft's exit was followed a week later by the departure of his deputy, Tim Jolly. Why there has been such a sudden flurry of activity I do not know, but an article in *Retail Week* magazine suggested that Mr Craft had left because he was frustrated by Spar's unwieldy bureaucracy. (Tautology! When was bureaucracy ever not unwieldy? Isn't it the whole point?) Apparently, strategic decisions have to be ratified by the organisation's National Guild Board, made up of directors from the seven sales areas and seven major Spar retailers, as well as the Spar main board. No wonder Mr Craft sailed to less turbulent waters, though one is forced to wonder why he took the job in the first place.

Spar represents something of a contradiction. To judge from

its stores, it is the most parochial and provincial of all the retailers I write about but in fact as a franchised brand Spar has international coverage which most of the big supermarket chains can only dream about. It is in fact the world's largest and most international food retailer, operating in 28 countries and across five continents. According to an article in *Checkout* magazine, International Spar reported a particularly strong performance in Ireland, Hungary, France, Eastern Europe, South Africa and Austria. Austria is obviously serious Spar territory. The retail group actually runs its own TV station there. Likely to have featured prominently on TV Spar this year was the 1999 International Spar annual conference which was held in Vienna in May. Over the past year or so, Spar has also extended its influence in the Baltic states opening new stores in Lithuania and Estonia.

Spar UK has itself been looking beyond national borders with the aim of increasing its presence in Scotland. Last year, it announced a link-up with Texaco to develop Spar-operated convenience stores at 29 Texaco petrol stations in Scotland. At about the same time, the retailer sought to raise its profile in Scotland with an advertising campaign featuring an Elvis lookalike and the strapline 'so near, so Spar, whoever you are'. In typical Spar style, every retailer which trades under the brand in Scotland contributed to the £400,000 campaign. But the retailer as yet has revealed no plans to launch its own UK TV station or to broadcast the ad nationally.

On the off-licence front, Spar last year was clearly in a bullish mood. In August 1998, Spar said in *The Grocer* magazine that it expected its wine sales to hit record levels during that year. Spar's wine sales, according to the report, had risen by 16% in the first 12 weeks of the financial year. A month later in *Off-Licence News* Spar restated its commitment to developing its off-licence offer. Trading director Keith Webb said that off-licence sales had grown by 14% over the past year. The retailer said that much of the development in wine had come in the £3.50 to £4 per bottle range.

It was thus no surprise to read that Spar was making the improvement of off-licence departments a key feature in a major store development programme launched earlier in 1999. The aim of the Millennium Store Package programme is to modernise the interiors and exteriors of all its 2,665 stores in the UK by the end of 2000. According to a report in *Off-Licence News*, the idea is to create more of a shop-in-shop feel with a change in ceiling height and differentiated lighting and flooring. Retailers will be asked to take revolutionary steps like displaying wines by country of origin and taking advantage of newly designed 'information graphics'. Even though there are three different levels of store upgrade available to Spar's retail members, all will be able to take advantage of the off-licence upgrade.

Spar clearly wants more of its retailers to regard themselves as wine merchants, offering a good range of wines in the right ambience. A case study published in *Checkout* magazine in 1998 arguably presents an ideal example to follow. The article focuses on wine tastings hosted by Steve and Alice Bockett at their Spar shop in Ringwood, Hampshire. The couple said they sold up to £800 worth of wine at the popular pre-Christmas tastings which they obviously take very seriously. They print some 500 customer invitations and offer four or five wines, typically in the £3.50 to £4.50 price bracket, for tasting. The tastings usually attract about 200 people and they get through about 60 bottles (= 360 glasses of wine – you work it out – but plainly no drunken orgy ensued). For Mr Bockett it is not just an opportunity to get customers to try new wines and sell more bottles. It helps to affirm the store's identity as a community business. 'People really like it,' he told *Checkout*. 'They see it almost as a social event, especially in the run-up to Christmas. All sorts of people come, even those you would not ordinarily associate with wine. And it makes people aware that we are serious about our off licence section,' he said. Mr Bockett also said they were considering running pre-summer tastings as well.

I consider this sort of initiative, which I would never have associated with this retailer, as truly a landmark achievement.

But it is important that Spar do not send out invitations solely to established customers. They must hire out-of-work actors to impersonate Oddbins employees and run the tastings, and they must distribute leaflets about the tastings – which must also offer prizes and the opportunity to pick up members of the opposite or same sex – to Oddbins and Majestic customers. Then we will really see Spar motor on the wine side.

Spar Landmark
32-40 Headstone Drive
Harrow
Middlesex HA3 5QT
Tel: 0181 863 5511
Fax: 0181 863 0603

AUSTRALIAN WINE RED

Hardys Bankside Shiraz 1997

By far the best red I've tasted at Spar. Good age, lovely rich fruit (savoury and spicy) and lovely tannins.

AUSTRALIAN WINE WHITE

Burraburra Hill Chardonnay 1997

Some food-friendly stickiness about the fruit but it needs food.

Lindemans Bin 65 Chardonnay 1998

A hugely elegant vintage, this, for a classic Aussie chardonnay. It has purpose, stealth, wit and warmth, and invites comparison with chardonnays daring to cost a lot more.

BULGARIAN WINE RED

Bulgarian Country Wine Cabernet Sauvignon & Cinsault NV

Ah, drinkability (just).

BULGARIAN WINE — WHITE

Bulgarian Country White, Slaviantzi NV

Hints at sweetness.

CHILEAN WINE — RED

Canepa Cabernet Sauvignon 1998

Good rich texture and harmony between tannins and fruit. Touch of sulphur was a bit obvious on the bottle I tried.

Canepa Merlot 1998

Juicy but has a pleasant savoury finish. Texture's great.

CHILEAN WINE — WHITE

Canepa Chilean Chardonnay 1998

Not one of Chile's most strikingly handsome chardonnays.

Chilean Chardonnay 1997

Chilean Sauvignon Blanc 1998

Nicely oily texture and richness to the fruit. Finishes well, if not as dryly as it might.

FRENCH WINE   RED

Claret NV   `11` `C`

Juicy and loose.

Cordier Chateau Le Cadet de Martinens, Margaux 1995   `13` `E`

Very good tannins holding some fair fruit. Too pricey, though.

Coteaux du Languedoc NV   `13` `B`

Bitter – did it lead a lousy childhood?

Cotes de Ventoux 1997   `13` `C`

Could be . . . but not quite . . .

Fitou NV, Spar   `12` `B`

The fruit scrambles to stay in touch with the acidity.

French Country VdP de l'Herault NV   `14` `C`

A solid party wine. Has character and will chill nicely.

Gamay VdP du Jardin de la France NV   `10` `C`

Juicy and semi-literate.

Gevrey-Chambertin Les Caves des Hautes Cotes 1994   `12` `G`

Has some inkling of earthy, truffley pinot but for thirteen pounds I want an emphatic wine, not its inkling.

FRENCH RED

Hautes Cotes de Beaune 1995 11 D

Uninspiring for seven quid.

Lussac St Emilion 1997 11 D

Too pricey for such veiled fruit.

Merlot, VdP d'Oc NV 14

Has some juicy cherry fruit, good nutty edge and tannins.

Oaked Merlot VdP d'Oc NV 14 C

Juicy, hint of leather, decent tannins, pleasant cherry finish.

Syrah VdP d'Oc 1997 13.5

Reasonably cheap glugging here.

VdP de la Cite de Carcassonne Red 1997 10

Almost disgusting. Very earthy.

Vin de Pays de l'Aude NV 12 B

Not very alert as it finishes.

FRENCH WINE WHITE

Chablis Union des Viticulteurs de Chablis
1997 13.5

Perfectly acceptable fruit, to an extent – but not to eight quid's worth.

French Country VdP de l'Herault White NV

Rusticity fructified.

French Country Wine NV (1 litre)

Grenache VdP d'Oc NV

Raw, rustic, rushed to crush.

Muscat de St Jean de Minervois (half bottle)

The best white wine bargain at Spar. A sweet, honeyed dessert wine of richness, layered delights and a lovely herby-treacle finish (though this is subtle – not strident). A lovely wine for blue cheese, fresh fruit and goat's cheese, or light after-dinner pastries.

Oaked Chardonnay NV

Oaked Chardonnay VdP d'Oc NV

Good rich fruit, handsome texture with a hint of ripeness and a solid fruity finish.

Pouilly Fuisse Les Vercheres Chardonnay 1996

Why does the label say chardonnay? Concession to new world habits? If so, it's a pity this learning didn't stretch to the fruit.

Rose d'Anjou, Spar

Sancerre Sarget 1998

Very drinkable, gently plump (rich, ripe vintage, the '98) and some pleasing fullness on the finish. Not classic but good.

Unoaked Chardonnay VdP d'Oc NV | 14.5 | C

Good balance and elemental harmony here. Good with food or mood.

VdP de la Cite de Carcassonne 1997 | 12 | B

Bit earthy and rustic.

Vin de Pays de l'Aude Blanc NV | 12 | B

Not advised for those of a nervous palate.

Vouvray Donatien Bahuaud 1997 | 12 | C

Very sweet and one-dimensional.

White Burgundy Chardonnay 1996 | 13 | D

Pleonastic (white burgundy can only be chardonnay) and medium pleasing.

GERMAN WINE   WHITE

Grans Fassian Riesling 1996 | 15 | D

Needs a few years to really shine but it has classic touches now.

HUNGARIAN WINE   RED

Danube Fruity Red | 9 | B

Pretty ugly – interesting paradox which isn't attractive in the throat.

Misty Mountain Merlot NV   `11` `C`

Called 'Misty', presumably, because the vigneron cried, when he tasted the wine, for what the winemakers had done with his grapes.

HUNGARIAN WINE   WHITE

Danube Country White NV   `13` `B`

A touch tarty.

Misty Mountain Chardonnay NV   `13` `C`

Touch of sweetness.

ITALIAN WINE   RED

Ariento Sangiovese del Rubicone NV   `12` `C`

Very ripe.

Barolo 'Costa di Bussia' 1994   `11` `G`

A lot of money for a wine which is going raisiny and ripe.

Chianti Chiantigiane 1997   `10` `C`

Chianti Classico Le Fioraie 1995   `13` `E`

Very mature and pruney – and the tannins are wearing through the fruit.

Montepulciano d'Abruzzo, Cantino Tollo 1998

`14` `C`

Very earthy cherries. Great with pasta.

Pasta Red NV

`10` `C`

Skinny fruit.

ITALIAN WINE   WHITE

Pasta White NV

`15.5` `C`

Superb little charmer. Accurately monikered, fresh, textured, touch classy.

Trebbiano d'Abruzzo 1997

`11` `C`

Raw grapes.

SOUTH AFRICAN WINE   RED

Chiwarra Pinotage 1998

`14.5` `C`

Very ripe and rampant but its youth has energy, richness, terrific tannins and a rousing finish. A great wine for big parties and casserole eaters.

Chiwarra Ruby Cabernet/Pinotage 1998

`11` `C`

Fruit juice with attitude (limp).

**Longridge Bay View Ruby Cabernet
Pinotage 1997** 13 D

Full, rubbery, rich and all-embracing.

South African Classic Red NV 11 C

Sweet-edged fruit of cloying anonymity.

Table Mountain Pinot Noir NV 10 C

Good frozen on a stick.

SOUTH AFRICAN WINE WHITE

Chiwarra Colombard/Sauvignon 1998 12.5 C

Curious sticky/crisp paradox which doesn't entirely sort itself
out on the finish.

Classic White Vintners Blend NV 14 C

Good smoked fish wine.

**Longridge Bay View Chenin Chardonnay
1997**   13.5 D

Some warmth to the fruit.

**South African Classic Chardonnay Lightly
Wooded 1998** 14 D

Well chilled with a plate of eel pie (or cockles), it'll do.

Table Mountain Chenin Blanc 1997   `12` `C`

Dull fruit here.

SPANISH WINE   RED

Campo Rojo Carinena NV   `13` `B`

Good chilled with a fish stew.

Perfect for Parties Red NV (1 litre)   `11` `B`

What sort of parties? Firing, burial, etc . . . Price band reflects
the 75cl equivalent.

Valencia Soft Red NV   `13` `B`

Yes, it's soft all right.

SPANISH WINE   WHITE

Campo Verde Carinena   `13` `B`

Very warm and fruity and needing spicy food to ignite.

Perfect for Parties White NV (1 litre)   `14` `B`

Like the label says (lively, cheap, sociable, fruity). Price band
reflects the 75cl price.

Valencia Dry White NV   `13` `B`

Dry and white about says it all. Basic fruit here.

FORTIFIED WINE

Old Cellar LBV Port 1994

Bit sweet and won't shine with food – which it must.

Old Cellar Ruby Port NV

An excellent fruity rich Port for ripe cheeses.

SPARKLING WINE/CHAMPAGNE

Marques de Prevel Champagne NV

One of the better grocery champagnes around, although the price edges towards the stiff as the wine's fruit edges towards the crisp.

THRESHER
(+ WINE RACK &
BOTTOMS UP)
& VICTORIA WINE
now known as
'FIRST QUENCH'

Companies take names very seriously nowadays. When Guinness and Grand Metropolitan merged in 1997 they spent much time and money deliberating over a new name, eventually coming up with Diageo, a name derived from the Greek word for world and the Latin word for day. According to the chairman, Tony Greener, 'because every day, all around the world, millions of people enjoy our brands, Diageo captures what this company is all about.' Well I never. Why, you yawn, mention this? Because the off-licence trade has also witnessed a colossal merger and after news of the marriage of Victoria Wine and Thresher I eagerly awaited news of what the merged group was going to call itself.

The company's management did not employ expensive branding consultants as Diageo had done but set to the task themselves and, possibly exhibiting a scarcity of classics scholars at board level, decided on the rather more prosaic First Quench which has a certain simple charm. The name suggests pre-eminence in the business of quenching – and the group is unquestionably the largest off-licence chain (and the largest retailer of champagne in

Europe) with 3,000 outlets and sales of around £1.3 billion –
but could it be that simple? Apparently not. Quench, so it has
been revealed, is derived from the first two letters of the words
quality, enjoyment and choice. Yep, I was also gobsmacked when
I heard that.

Well, choice is certainly something you have with First
Quench. Individually, the two chains were launching new retail
concepts – sub-brands is what marketing jargon calls the practice
– like they were going out of style, so the merged group has a
remarkably broad range of identities. Ironically, the name which
the public will least associate with the group is the ingenious
moniker First Quench which will not be appearing above any
shop door of the company whatever other guises it might take
(Victoria Wine, Victoria Wine Cellars, Bottoms Up, Thresher,
Haddows, Drinks Cabin, Wine Rack, Martha's Vineyard, Firkin
Off-Licence, Drinks Direct, Huttons, and HomeRun the last
time I looked).

In last year's *Streetplonk*, I reported that the merger had been
proposed but it had not yet been ratified. After the customary
lengthy investigations, the merger was officially ratified by
Trade and Industry Minister, Peter Mandelson, in October
1998 before other investigations brought his ratifying career
to an abrupt halt. First Quench's competitor, Parisa, another
company which had spent much time deciding what to call
itself, had opposed the merger.

A report in *Off-Licence News* in October suggested that the
merger had been justified in the light of financial performance
of both chains prior to their marriage. Victoria Wine's profits
and turnover had been flat in the year to the end of August
1998, while Thresher reported that like-for-like sales had fallen
by 1.2% in the six months to the end of August. Victoria Wine's
owners, Allied Domecq, and Whitbread, which owns Thresher,
said the partnership would be 'earnings enhancing.' (Ye Gods,
why don't they just say 'make more money'?!) However, judging
from Allied Domecq's results for the next six months early profit
gains were not forthcoming. According to *The Grocer* magazine

in May 1999, the company recorded a profit of £3 million from its 50% share in First Quench in the six months to the end of February 1999, £4 million less than it had made from Victoria Wine in the same period a year earlier when it had been a separate concern. The group attributed the shortfall to lower sales, cost inflation and the disruption of the merger. Allied Domecq's pubs and off-licences then became an acquisition target for the pubs group, Punch Taverns. As this introduction goes to press (some months before I finish the wine listing sections), this area has become somewhat muddied and I confess to feeling mightily confused. Allied Domecq rejected the Punch Taverns bid (£2.925 billion) for its retail businesses in favour of the lower bid from Whitbread of £2.8 billion. It preferred the 'lower risk and shorter timetable' of the Whitbread offer. It seems as though First Quench may become a wholly-owned subsidiary of Whitbread. Or not? By the time this book comes out, it will have been settled.

Indeed, it appears that the formation of the First Quench partnership is the beginning rather than the end of the story. In May, it was suggested in *Off-Licence News* that Whitbread would possibly take over full ownership of First Quench and that it would eventually be floated or sold off. Nader Haghighi, the Parisa boss so opposed to the merger in the first place, was also thought to be interested in putting together a bid for the group (pie in the sky this latter notion, in my view).

Job losses and store closures are one of the least palatable aspects of the creation of a giant like First Quench and I was naturally anxious to see how my acquaintances in the two wine buying departments would fare during what a new management refers to as 'bedding down' and which usually signifies precisely the opposite to many employees. I was pleased to read in *Off-Licence News* in October 1998 that Kim Tidy, a veteran of Thresher (and one of the most able wine buyers in the industry), had been named trading manager for wine for the group. But Victoria Wine's buying and marketing director, Richard Lowe, lost his job in preference to his Thresher counterpart, Ralph

Hayward. Reports last year suggested that some 300 stores would be closed and 1,000 jobs would be axed as a result of the merger.

There was at least some positive news for Thresher staff with the introduction of a new qualification for off-licence managers. About 50 Thresher managers were set to be the first recipients of the certificate, according to *Off-Licence News*, with 400 more to follow in 1999. Trainees have to complete Threshers Pathway for Training and Progression before they attend a five-day residential course. After this they have to complete a business plan for their branch which is then assessed by an area manager. The certificate is validated by the National Licensee Awarding Body, part of the British Institute of Innkeeping. The company hopes it will become a benchmark for the industry. However, while managers seemed to be faring well there were less to cheer among the rank and file when First Quench announced in November that it was ending its pay and conditions agreements with USDAW, the shopworkers' union. Actually, only about 1,000 of the chain's 20,000 staff were union members.

One early casualty of the merger was Victoria Wine's gift delivery service, Poste Haste, which was axed shortly after the deal was agreed. Drinks Direct, Thresher's home delivery operation, became the home delivery arm for the merged group. At £5.99 per delivery, Drinks Direct is incidentally £1 more expensive than Poste Haste. First Quench is clearly wasting no time in enhancing those earnings. Staying with home shopping, First Quench introduced the Wine Rack Direct catalogue the following month which it hoped would be seen as the Next Directory for wine consumers. In the *FT*, First Quench's direct marketing executive, Nicola Ferguson, said that the catalogue has a coffee table feel to it which you would think might make it somewhat unwieldy.

There is no mystery about why First Quench is raising its profile in this market. According to the *FT*, the home delivery wine market is worth around £200 million a year and at the moment the main players are Wines Direct, the company behind the Sunday Times Wine Club, and the Wine Society. The Wine Rack Direct 52-page tome lists around 770 wines with photographs and tasting notes and is available to customers for the price of £3 at Wine Rack, Bottoms Up and Thresher Wine Shops. In a related move, First Quench announced in January that it was testing a wine party scheme in London and the Midlands. As with ladies' undies and Tupperware, hosts are recruited to organise parties where invited guests can buy wine.

Precisely what First Quench plans to do with all its retail brands has not been made fully clear, but it was reported in January that the Victoria Wine Cellars stores were to be integrated with Threshers Wine Rack chain. It was also reported that First Quench might convert some standard off-licences in Scotland to smaller versions of the Bottoms Up concept.

It also appears that Victoria Wine's Martha's Vineyard drinks superstore remains part of corporate strategy. Last November, the company opened its second Martha's Vineyard store at the Cribbs Causeway Retail Park in Bristol. At 5,500 sq ft, this store is larger than the first Martha's Vineyard in Barnet. Seven more Martha's Vineyard outlets are in the pipeline and the company has plans for a chain of around 50 stores. In April, Victoria Wine opened its first concourse store at Victoria Station. The store is operated by the station retail specialists, Select Service Partner, which had already been operating an unbranded off-licence on the site. Victoria Wine was reportedly looking to open further station outlets in the coming year. Another departure for Victoria Wine was the opening last year of off-licence sections within Alldays convenience stores. The c-store company was also opening separate but unbranded off-licence sections in some of its stores and intended to compare the performance of the two.

The first news about redundancies at First Quench concerned bottles rather than bodies. It was reported in *Off-Licence News* in November that the company planned to cut some 500 wines from its range which had swelled at that stage to 1,450 different bottles. The cull was expected to be completed by March 1999. In fact, by May 1999 the wine range had been cut from 1,400 to 800. The company said in *Off-Licence News* that the cull had not diminished choice but had simply eliminated the poorer wines. The reduced range now comprises 54% red wine and Kim Tidy said he would not be surprised if red wines account for 75% of the range in five years' time.

My own feelings about this are motivated by two considerations. I do not despise size, merely for the fact of it. Size creates more buying clout, and can give the wine department buyers more confidence and diversity of choice. However, I always felt that at the old Victoria Wine they were playing around the edges of the problem, the heart of which is surely the quality of staff and layout of the individual stores, while at the old Thresher I thought the quality of the shops never matched the expertise and ambitions of the departmental wine buyers. My hope is that the merger of two chains with the same problem doesn't compound it but finally solves it. In an interview with the wine trade magazine *Harper's*, senior wine buyer Matthew Dickinson said 'How far the (shop) manager wants to progress depends on personal commitment but we do provide training programmes which combine learning with selling skills. We're still working on this area and know it's crucial, but it's costly.'

I want readers to go to First Quench operated outlets, whatever the name on the fascia, and be confronted by bright staff and bonny wines. The latter end of this bargain the buyers are managing to get right, though I would like to see more solid value around £3.99 and less gimmicky names, but it's the directors who oversee the shops and those shop managers (whose commitment is a personal affair rather than an entrenched corporate dynamic) who need to ensure that these glitter like never before. See to this, and you will have real competition for the supermarkets.

Is this remotely achievable, however, with no women wine buyers at First Quench? True, there was the indefatigably charming Nicola Harvey (ex-VW) responsible for public relations but she recently moved to something called Strategic Projects, Jo Locke went on maternity leave (promising to return to PR afterwards) and Lulie Halstead disappeared to have a baby, all of which leaves eight men to buy the wine and they enjoy a breadth of precisely delineated responsibility unmatched by any retailer I know of. I have already mentioned Kim Tidy, trading manager, but there is a wine development manager, Jonathan Butt, and a trio of senior wine buyers: Julian Twaites (Champagne is one of his areas), Mark Jarman (amongst other things he handles Retsina and Kosher wines) and Matthew Dickinson (who has several things to concern him including Vin de Pays and wine boxes). This leaves two wine buyers: Paul Liversedge (who has to taste Lambrusco and no-alcohol wines in his portfolio) and Andy Brown (who can include Wales in his remit but not British wines).

There is also Spike Garrett who runs the computers (I think). Mr Garrett also wields a nifty corkscrew and tells jokes at wine tastings. But he has a capacious beard and would look absurd in a Nicole Farhi trouser suit and Maud Frizon slingbacks. These lapses apart, First Quench's wine buying department has flair and taste and the evidence of this is in the entries which follow.

First Quench (Victoria Wine, Victoria Wine Cellars, Bottoms Up, Thresher, Haddows, Drinks Cabin, Wine Rack, Martha's Vineyard, Firkin Off-Licence, Drinks Direct, Huttons, HomeRun)
Sefton House
42 Church Road
Welwyn Garden City
Herts AL8 6PJ
Tel: 01707 328244
Fax: 01707 371398

First Quench Retailing Limited (the old Victoria Wine HQ)
Dukes Court
Duke Street
Woking
Surrey GU21 5XL
Tel: 01483 715066
Fax: 01483 755234

See page 245 for Victoria Wine wines listing. Thresher (Wine Rack & Bottoms Up) follow.

SEE STOP PRESS SECTION AT END OF BOOK FOR LAST-MINUTE ADDITIONS OR UPDATES TO THIS RETAILER'S RANGE.

ARGENTINIAN WINE — WHITE

Correas Torrontes/Chardonnay 1997   `10` `C`

So cosmetic!

Norton Torrontes, Mendoza 1999   `13` `C`

AUSTRALIAN WINE — RED

Cornerstone Barossa Grenache Shiraz Mourvedre 1997   `15` `E`

Blasts you with such vigour and explosive shrapnel of shredded fruit you need a bib to drink it. The rich tannins are free at last to strike. But it's a big bear of a wine with a very cuddly heart.

Heritage Cabernet Malbec 1995   `13` `E`

Nanya Estate Malbec/Ruby Cabernet 1997   `14` `C`

Nanya Estate Malbec/Ruby Cabernet 1998   `14.5` `C`

Almonds, plums, and a baked soft-fruit edge make this a plump specimen, food-friendly and mood-friendly.

Oxford Landing Merlot 1998   `14.5` `D`

A solid merlot rather than a thrilling one, it has some charm and propriety, manners and merlot credentials.

Primo Estate Adelaide Shiraz 1996   15   E

Cannot be drunk without food or a big grin on the face. This definitely interferes with conventional tasting procedures but then so does the wine! It's a bomb of emulsion thick savoury fruit with a baked pie crust edge. Extraordinary. Wine Rack stores.

Red Cliffs Reserve Black Label Cabernet Sauvignon 1996   15.5   D

Red Cliffs Shiraz 1997   16   C

Best vintage yet. In its '97 manifestation, it's rich and soupy yet with remarkably well tailored tannins. A terrific wine.

Riddoch 'Limited Release' Coonawarra Shiraz 1996   15   D

Samuel's Bay Pinot Noir 1997   13   D

Samuels Bay Grenache 1997   16   D

One of the most concentrated grenaches I've tasted. Plummy, cigar-edged, perfumed, rich, very free-flowing yet delicate, this is an immensely quaffable food wine of considerable charm.

Samuels Bay Malbec, Padthaway 1995   15   D

Soupy and juicy and great with Indian food.

St Hallett Barossa Shiraz 1997   13   E

Too juicy for eight quid.

St Hallett Grenache 1996   15   E

Tatachilla Grenache Shiraz 1998   16   D

This estate has come on so much since it changed ownership.

A decade ago I saw grapes destined for Tatachilla swollen with irrigated water but not the beauties which went into this bargain blend. The wine has style, bravura, loads of fruit but is never silly or too juicy. The tannins are temperate and tasty. With increasing Oz prices, this is a sane specimen in a mad world.

Tollana Red, SE Australia NV

Wynn's Coonawarra Shiraz 1996

Superbly classy and rich. Hints of mint cling to the deeply textured (denim and corduroy) fruit (plums, cherries and black-currants) and the sheer cheek of the fruit, its bounce yet gravitas, is terrific – the finish is syrup of figs.

AUSTRALIAN WINE WHITE

Black Noble de Bortolie NV (half bottle)

Cough mixture meets old, molasses-rich sherry. A remarkably thick pudding wine to handsomely partner Christmas pudding or to pour over ice cream. It would be a superb accompaniment to *tarte tatin*.

Cullen Margaret River Sauvignon Blanc/Semillon 1997 `14` `F`

Very expensive but reassuringly individual and fruity. Rich yet never overblown, quiet yet far from shy, it has an inner core of charm and impressive sippability. Wine Rack stores.

David Traeger Verdelho, Victoria 1998 `16` `E`

A real spicy treat! Lovely pineapple/citrus edging to ripe peach and pear fruit. Great quaffing and oriental food wine.

Jacobs Creek Dry Riesling 1997 `14` `C`

Katnook Sauvignon Blanc, Coonawarra 1997 `14` `E`

Lenswood Adelaide Hills Sauvignon Blanc, Tim Knappstein 1997 `16` `F`

Extreme elegance here – like a haut couture creation: hand sewn, silky, beautifully formed and well fitting. Wine Rack only.

Oxford Landing Estate Viognier 1996 `14` `D`

Gentle rather than gorgeous. But the apricot edge is a trimming as opposed to the whole cut of the thing.

Oxford Landing Sauvignon Blanc 1999 `14.5` `C`

Very fresh and perky. Good finish to an elegant wine.

Penfolds Barossa Valley Semillon Chardonnay 1997 `16.5` `D`

Love its richness and utter regality. It really lords it over other chardonnay blends.

Pewsey Vale Riesling 1997 `16` `D`

The satin texture is one thing, the nigh-classic aroma is another (something no European riesling acquires so young), and the finish is yet another. Even so, you can cellar it for five more years and who knows if perfection won't emerge?

Red Cliffs Estate Colombard Chardonnay 1997 `14` `C`

Red Cliffs Sauvignon Blanc 1997 `14` `C`

Riddoch Chardonnay, Coonawarra 1996 | 16 | D

Super mouth-filling plumpness of ripe fruit here, hint of caramel cream even, but the acidity surges alongside in support and the finish is regal. Very classy wine.

Samuels Bay Riesling, Eden Valley 1997 | 16 | D

Very rich, thick fruit with a touch of exoticism which will be brilliant with oriental food.

Samuels Bay Sauvignon Blanc 1997 | 13.5 | D

Thomas Mitchell Marsanne 1996 | 16 | C

Terrific oily fruit of substance, wit and staying power. Supreme idea to match with Thai fish cakes, scallops, squid etc.

Tollana Unoaked Chardonnay 1999 | 15.5 | C

More attentive to the purity of chardonnay fruit, unmasked by wood, than a million Chablis at three times the price. New World richness, yes, but it's subtle.

BULGARIAN WINE   RED

Copper Crossing Red NV | 14 | B

Simple fruity quaffing. Good with food, too. Has a dry edge.

Domaine Boyar Premium Oaked Cabernet Shumen 1997 | 13.5 | C

Domaine Boyar Premium Reserve Cabernet Sauvignon 1996 `14` `C`

Very approachable.

Domaine Boyar Premium Reserve Merlot 1996 `14` `C`

Hints of leather and a subtle spiciness.

Iambol Vintage Blend Cabernet/Merlot, Domaine Boyar 1997 `14` `B`

Premier Oaked Cabernet Sauvignon 1997 `13.5` `C`

Premier Oaked Merlot 1997 `14.5` `C`

Touch more meat, aroma and tannin in the oaked version. A good casserole wine.

Premier Reserve Cabernet Sauvignon 1996 `14.5` `C`

An approachable level of rich, soft fruit which strikes a handsome dry note as it quits the throat.

Premier Reserve Merlot 1996 `14` `C`

Touch fruity on the finish but some worthy fruit on the middle of the palate and a pleasing perfume.

Russe Country Red Cabernet/Cinsault NV `13.5` `B`

BULGARIAN WINE WHITE

Boyar Muskat & Ugni Blanc NV `11` `B`

Copper Crossing Dry White NV

Lovely glugging fruit here: crisp, clean, medium-bodied fruit of great charm.

**Domaine de Boyar Targovischte
Chardonnay 1997** `12` `B`

More like a sauvignon than anything.

CHILEAN WINE RED

Cono Sur Cabernet Sauvignon, Rapel 1998

Unusually gruff-voiced, gravely Chilean cabernet – but high class and very accomplished.

Errazuriz Reserve Syrah 1997 `17.5` `E`

Runs away with the imagination – has leather, spice, tobacco, chocolate and cassis. And it's all sprinkled with lively yet warm tannins. Wine Rack shops only.

La Palma Cabernet/Merlot 1997

So compellingly complex and gluggable you scrutinise the price tag with as much astonishment as you behold the wonderful fruit.

La Palmeria Cabernet/Merlot 1998 `16` `C`

Very dark and savoury. A big-shouldered wine which pulls its weight with food.

Las Colinas Cabernet 1998

Dry, vegetal, touch stalky and typically rich on the throat.

Santa Ines Legado de Armida Cabernet Sauvignon Reserve 1997

Almost dainty, at first sip, then it turns ferociously eloquent and rich in the back of the gullet and shows great dry character and teeth-clenchingly classy tannins.

Santa Ines Legardo de Armida Reserve Malbec 1997

Rich, gentle and powerful, very dry and lingering. Wine Rack and Bottoms Up only.

Santa Ines Legardo de Armida Reserve Merlot 1997

17 D

Fantastic coffee tannins and rich, complex fruit. Wonderful texture and richness. Wine Rack and Bottoms Up only.

Valdivieso Malbec 1998

15 C

Malbec as smooth and plump as it comes picked.

CHILEAN WINE · WHITE

Casa Lapostolle Sauvignon Blanc 1997

16 C

Concha y Toro Casillero del Diablo Chardonnay 1997

Not as gracious as previous vintages, but still a fair chardonnay under a fiver.

Cono Sur Gewurztraminer 1997

Bit florid and blowsy.

Las Colinas Sauvignon Blanc 1998   14   C

Hint of grass tickles the nose, then gets richer and fatter as the fruit meets the palate.

Santa Ines Legardo de Armida Reserve Chardonnay 1997   17.5   D

Such vast richness of tone, elegance and sheer gorgeous texture – a world class wine at an absurd price. Wine Rack and Bottoms Up only.

Soleca Semillon, Colchagua Valley 1997   16.5   C

Fabulously rich fruit here: ripe melon, raspberries, limes and pineapples. And it has a plastic, taint-free cork!

FRENCH WINE   RED

Abbotts Cumulus Shiraz Minervois 1998   15   D

The polish to the herbs and Midi-mannered earthiness is terrific.

Beaujolais AC Regional Classics 1997   13.5   C

The label speaks true: a soft fruity red. No mention, though, of the palate's discovery of a pleasant dry cherry finish.

Beaujolais Villages Duboeuf 1997   13   D

Pushy name, not so pushy fruit, adventurous price.

Chateau Cap de Faugeres, Cotes de Castillon 1993   15.5   E

Chateau d'Aiguilhe, Cotes de Castillon 1994

15 E

A fat mouthful with a rascally finish and edge of mannered leatheriness and good tannins. Wine Rack and Bottoms Up only.

Chateau Langoiran Cuvee Classique 1996

13.5 E

Juicy (unusually so for a Cotes de Bordeaux) – but it does go dry-as-dust on the finish.

Chateau Mercier Oak Aged 1er Cotes de Bourg 1996

14.5 E

Saucy and ripe – yet has some dignified tannins. Thus, tenacity is conferred.

Chateau Puy Bardens, 1er Cotes de Bordeaux 1996

13.5 C

Chateau Puy Bardens Cuvee Prestige, 1er Cotes de Bordeaux 1996

12.5 E

Chateau Rose d'Orion Montagne, St Emilion 1996

14.5 D

Chateau Sauvage Premier Cotes de Bordeaux 1997

15 D

Excellent claret here where the bristly tannins are controlled by textured classy fruit.

Chateau Suau, 1er Cotes de Bordeaux 1996 (oaked)

13 D

Chateau Suau, 1er Cotes de Bordeaux 1997 (unoaked)

13.5 D

Very firm and fruity, not remotely like claret – it's quaffable.

Claret Regional Classic, Sichel NV `14` `C`

Cotes de Beaune Villages 1996 `12` `E`

Strains to portray itself as wine rather than fruit juice.

**Cotes du Rhone Chateau du Grand
Prebois 1995** `14` `D`

Lot of well-cooked meat here.

Cotes du Rhone Villages Les Faisans 1998 `14` `C`

Very smooth, unhurried, calm and fruity performer. Not a dry
eye in the house.

**Cotes du Rhone Villages Vinsobres,
Domaine de la Bicarelle 1995** `14` `D`

Very soft and juicy, unusual for a Vinsobres. Perhaps a touch
expensive, too. Wine Rack and Bottoms Up stores.

Cotes du Ventoux La Mission 1997 `14` `C`

Good herby fruit with a touch of the sun.

Dark Horse Cahors 1998 `14` `C`

An attempt to civilise the black wine of Cahors.

Fitou Special Reserve 1997 `14.5` `C`

Ripe yet dry. Good chilled.

Fleurie Georges Duboeuf 1998 `11` `E`

Fleurie Regional Classics 1998 `13.5` `D`

Very juicy and drinkable with a hint of character – but seven
quid? That takes some swallowing.

French Connection Cabernet/Syrah 1998 `14` `C`

Juicy but dry to finish.

**L'Esprit de Chevalier, Pessac Leognan
1994** `13.5` `G`

**La Demoiselle de Sociando, Haut Medoc
1995** `13.5` `F`

**Les Allees de Cantemerle, Haut Medoc
1995** `13` `E`

Merlot Bordeaux, Lurton 1996 `13` `C`

Mont Tauch Old Bush Vines Carignan 1998 `13` `C`

Very juicy.

Morgon Domaine des Cotes de Douby 1998 `13.5` `D`

Interesting fatness of stretched, fleshy fruit. Young, yes, and
pertly cherry-edged . . . but in two years? Maybe great.

Morgon Duboeuf 1997 `13` `D`

**Moulin-a-Vent Domaine de la Tour de
Bief 1996** `12` `E`

**Oak Aged Cotes du Rhone, Gabrielle
Meffre 1997** `15.5` `C`

Red Burgundy Vergy 1997 `12` `C`

Fruit juice.

Second de Durfort, Margaux 1994 `13` `E`

FRENCH WINE   WHITE

Chablis Regional Classics 1997   `12.5` `E`

Not eight quid's worth of fruit, I feel.

Chablis Vieilles Vignes, Defaix 1996   `11` `F`

Eleven pounds? Pull the other one.

Chablis Vieilles Vignes, La Cuvee
Exceptionelle, Defaix 1997   `12.5` `G`

Seventeen pounds! Incredible. Wine Rack and Bottoms Up
shops only.

Chateau Bonnet Entre Deux Mers 1998   `12` `D`

Touch muddled.

Chateau Bonnet Oak Aged Entre Deux
Mers 1996   `13` `E`

Too much wood for the paucity of fruit.

Chateau de Tariquet Chardonnay 1998   `14` `D`

A posh version of Cotes de Gascogne. Wine Rack and Bottoms
Up only.

Chateau Filhot Sauternes 1990   `15` `H`

Lovely burnt butter, honey, nuts and creme brulee fruit. A
pudding wine of elegance and distinction.

Chateau Petit Moulin Blanc, Bordeaux 1998   `12.5` `D`

A little less muddled than Chateau Bonnet.

Colombard Sauvignon Blanc au Loubet Vignoble Gascogne 1998

13.5 | C

Crisp and appley.

Domaine Laroche Chardonnay 'Tete de Cuvee' 1996

14 | D

Domaine Zind Humbrecht Clos Jebsal Pinot Gris 1996

17 | H

Sheer apricot heaven, a hint of honey, butter, lemon curd and caramel. This is pinot gris as an art form. Wine Rack stores.

Domaine Zind Humbrecht Vieilles Vignes Pinot Gris 1996

16.5 | G

The aroma is gentle smoke and butterscotch, the fruit is apricot with a touch of lemon zest, the finish is toffee and fresh hard fruit (some kind of exotic pear) and the whole construct is exuberant and hugely classy. Young still, and has ten years of exciting life. Wine Rack stores.

'Garden Valley' Chardonnay, VdP du Jardin de la France 1997

15 | C

James Herrick Chardonnay VdP d'Oc 1998

16.5 | C

Such delicacy of richness and toasty, nutty finish. Quite deliciously daring!

Le Vieux Mas Marsanne Viognier VdP d'Oc 1998

15 | C

Dry with a hint of minerals and fruit. Good smoked fish wine.

Macon-Lugny Saint-Pierre, Bouchard Pere 1996

12 | D

Muscadet Cotes de Grandlieu 1998 `13` `C`

Be okay with oysters.

Pouilly-Vinzelles Bouchard Pere 1996 `10` `E`

Riesling Wintzenheim Zind Humbrecht 1997 `14` `E`

Rich – but young. Give it four or five years to reach 18 points.
Wine Rack only.

**Riesling Zind Humbrecht Clos Hauserer
1997** `14` `G`

For fans of ZH solely. Rather young and in need of seeing a few
years of life. Wine Rack shops only.

Rivers Meet White Bordeaux 1997 `11` `C`

Bit dullish.

Tequirat Cotes de Gascogne 1998 `14` `C`

Exotic touches to this fresh, fruity, impishly refreshing wine.

Tokay Pinot Gris, Turckheim 1998 `13.5` `D`

Needs another eighteen months to rouse the apricots in the bottle
and raise the rating to 16.5 points.

Turckheim Gewurztraminer 1998 `16` `D`

Classic, spicy, rich, warm, immediate rosy/lychee/strawberry
fruit. Great throat refresher and plate accompanist.

Turckheim Pinot Blanc 1998 `14.5` `C`

I love the texture of this ripe, appley/pear (subtle touches, these),
richly intentioned wine. It's an individual wine of character.

GERMAN WINE WHITE

Kendermann Dry Riesling 1998 `12.5` `C`

This even dares to say 'Vineyard Selection' on the label, as though this coveys anything unusual. Where do they imagine we think the grapes come from? The greengrocer's? Well, come to think of it . . .

Piesporter Michelsberg QbA 1997 `10` `B`

Tokay Pinot Gris Herrenweg, Zind Humbrecht 1997 `16.5` `G`

So rich and roasted-honeyed that it whips the taste buds into peaks. Is it sweet? No. Is it dry? No way. Other categories refuse to accept it either. Perhaps goat's cheese and fruit are its best pals. Wine Rack only.

HUNGARIAN WINE WHITE

AK 28 Sauvignon Blanc 1998 `13` `C`

Curious squashed fruit finish from an austere-seeming overtone aromatically.

AK 68 Pink Pinot Gris 1998 `11` `C`

Odd and oddly unsatisfactory on the finish.

Cool Ridge Pinot Noir Rosé 1998 `13.5` `C`

Rather tasty and good with food. Wine Rack and Bottoms Up shops only.

Hilltop Gewurztraminer Slow Fermented 1997

The '98 will be much better!

ITALIAN WINE RED

Amarone della Valpolicella Classico 1993

A treat for Christmas lunch. A wine as variegated and spicy, rolling and raunchy, as the fowl's stuffing. Wine Rack shops only.

Caramia Negroamaro del Salento 1996

Has that wonderful Italian sense of earthy fun and fruit with an underlying deadliness of purpose: great with food! Wine Rack stores.

Cecchi Sangiovese 1998

Meatier, brisker, fruitier and altogether more charming than many a Chianti.

Rosso Montalcino, Casanova di Neri 1997

A lot of money. You get juice and gobbets of rich earth. Wine Rack only.

Salice Salento Vallone 1996

Totally prepared for food.

Trulli Primitivo 1997

Spicy, warm, herbal, rich, yet has a stealth-of-foot deftness as it quits the throat. Generous quaffing here and food-friendliness.

Zagara Sangiovese Syrah 1997

Chianti meets the Clare Valley in this Sicilian production of jammy ripeness.

ITALIAN WINE   WHITE

Falerio Pilastri Saladini 1998

Has the nervous finish of Italian fish wine.

Trulli Chardonnay Salento 1998   16   C

Delicate progression of richness yet delicacy courses over the taste buds here, leaving one refreshed and panting for more. It would be easy to quaff this wine too quickly and miss its abundant charms as it trips, with variegated steps, down the throat.

Verdicchio dei Castelli di Jesi Verbacco 1998   14   C

Nicely crisp but with an underlying fruity flow.

NEW ZEALAND WINE   RED

Church Road Cabernet Sauvignon/Merlot 1997

Bit expensive for admittedly drinkable fruit – nine quid gives you something to think about.

Felton Road Pinot Noir, Otago 1997 10 G

Sweet robbery. Wine Rack only.

Montana Reserve Merlot 1997 14 E

Expensive but a very good stab at a reserve merlot – aroma, leather, touch of spice, good texture and some satisfying length on the finish. Nine quid, though? Well . . .

NEW ZEALAND WINE WHITE

Azure Bay Chardonnay/Semillon 1998 14 C

Great with a Chinese takeaway.

Church Road Chardonnay 1998 16 E

Gorgeous price, true, but then so is the fruit. It has great smoky flavour and texture.

Cooks Gisborne Chardonnay 1997 13 D

Corbans Private Reserve Chardonnay, Gisborne 1995 16 E

It's the creamy integration of wood and fruit, which lingers on the taste buds most deliciously, which give the wine its considerable finesse (yet richness). Not at Thresher Wine Shops.

Dashwood Sauvignon Blanc, Marlborough 1997 15.5 D

Dry honey, gooseberry jam – luscious and rather ornate.

Montana Reserve Chardonnay 1998   15 E

Nothing reserved about the fruit as it hits the palate. Not elegant but magically entertaining.

Montana Reserve Gewurztraminer 1998   15 E

Melon, peaches and raspberries – delicious.

Nobilo White Cloud Muller-Thurgau/
Sauvignon Blanc 1997   10 C

Oyster Bay Sauvignon Blanc 1998   16 D

Quite lively richness yet restrained fluency of rippling fruit. Wine Rack and Bottoms Up shops only.

Palliser Estate Chardonnay 1995   15.5 E

Villa Maria Riesling 1998   15.5 D

Lovely now but in two or three years? Maybe 17 or 18 points. Terrific lilting fruit on the finish.

PORTUGUESE WINE   RED

Bright Brothers Douro Red 1996   13.5 C

Finishes a touch juicily for a fiver.

Dom Ferraz Dao 1997   16.5 C

Fabulous tufted texture and soft, ripe, curvaceous fruit. It really wraps itself round the taste buds. Quite gorgeously quaffable and delicious.

Espiga Red, Estremadura 1997   12 B

Fiuza Cabernet Sauvignon 1997   14 C

Chilled, great with fish. Warmer, great with meat and veg. In a glass, amusing to contemplate. On the palate, fresh and plummy and enjoyable.

Pedras do Monte 1998   16 C

From the terrific '98 vintage, this superb example of rich, balanced fruit offers bargain drinking. The tannins are decent yet very soft, savoury and smooth.

Ramada Red 1998   12.5 B

Juicier than previous vintages. Odd, considering how rich the '98 vintage in Portugal was.

Terra Boa Tras o Montes 1998   14.5 C

Tannins get going eventually alongside some warm, rich fruit. Has some character to it, this wine.

Terra Boa Vinho Tinto 1997   14 C

ROMANIAN WINE   RED

River Route Limited Edition Merlot 1996   15 C

Cherries, hint of leather, savoury finish. Great glugging here.

River Route Pinot Noir 1998   14 C

More pinot-like in perfume and in its lush, feral aftertaste than many a Cotes de Beaune at three times the price.

ROMANIAN WINE WHITE

River Route Limited Edition Chardonnay 1997

A thick, sticky, very beetle-browed chardonnay, with an acquired jammy richness. It must have rich food to be palatable – like tarragon chicken, prawn risotto, moules with lemon grass and chillies.

SOUTH AFRICAN WINE RED

Cape View Cinsaut/Shiraz 1998

Hmm . . . Took some getting, that 14 points. At £4.49 the wine is pricey. However, it's honest, dry, cherry-ripe and quaffable. But I itch to knock 70p off the price tag.

Oak Village Cabernet Sauvignon 1997 [13] [C]

Signature Cinsaut 1997

Such engaging warmth and richness and soft texture you wonder if it has a real hearth but it strikes cinder-hot and spicy on the finish. Wine Rack stores only.

Villiera Pinot Noir G & G Reserve 1997 [13] [E]

Wine Rack stores.

Winelands Cabernet Sauvignon/Franc, Stellenbosch 1997 [13.5] [D]

SOUTH AFRICAN WINE   WHITE

African Legend Sauvignon Blanc 1998   `13` `C`

Finishes on spindly legs – a bit.

Capells Court Chardonnay 1998   `16` `D`

Hint of spicy melon on the finish rounds off a rousing performance from a gorgeously textured and tightly woven specimen of top notch quaffing.

Capells Court Sauvignon Blanc 1998   `14.5` `D`

Lovely rich, rousing finish. Not classic, but a terrific food wine.

Carisbrook Chenin/Chardonnay 1999   `14` `C`

Rich and warm and needs oriental food.

'Deetlefs' Semillon 1997   `13.5` `E`

Pricey for the simplicity of the style.

**Delheim 'New Release' Chenin Blanc,
Stellenbosch 1996**   `15.5` `D`

Hartenberg 'Occasional' Auxerrois 1997   `16` `D`

Tremendous flavour and style here. A quirkily rich, chardonnay-style wine of complexity and real lengthy flavour. A thought-provokingly fruity wine. Not at Thresher Wine Shops.

**Hartenberg 'Occasional' Bush Vine Chenin
Blanc 1997**   `15.5` `D`

Hartenberg 'Occasional' Pinot Blanc 1997 `15` `D`

Interesting fruit here: creamy yet crisp. How it achieves this paradox I cannot say but the taste buds revel in it.

Hartenberg 'Occasional' Semillon 1997 `16` `D`

Vigour, vim, veracity, virtue – it offers the gamut of princely charms and offers them in a flood of controlled, well-refined richness and depth. Balanced, bonny wine. Not at Thresher Wine Shops.

Hartenberg Weisser Riesling, Stellenbosch 1997 `13` `D`

L'Avenir Chardonnay 1997 `14` `E`

Woody and winsome. Wine Rack and Bottoms Up only.

Savanha Barrel Fermented Chardonnay 1998 `14.5` `D`

Bit too chewy and rich for the faint-palated but with Thai food it would be unput-downable. Wine Rack and Bottoms Up only.

Signal Hill Barrel Fermented Chenin 1997 `16` `C`

Brilliant vanillary fruit, woody, gently rich, food friendly and imbued with great charm. Real style here.

Spice Route Long Walk Sauvignon Blanc 1998 `16` `D`

Fabulous fruit: juicy and ripe, yet subtle and clinging.

'The Collection' Chenin Blanc, Bellingham 1997 `15.5` `C`

'The Collection' Semillon, Bellingham 1997   15.5   C

Villiera Blanc Fume, Paarl 1997   13.5   D

Villiera Chardonnay 1997   16   E

Delicious vanilla edges to the smoky fruit. A really terrific partner for posh fish like scallop in cream sauce.

Villiera Chenin Blanc 1997   15   C

SPANISH WINE   RED

**Agramont Merlot Tempranillo, Navarra
1996**   14.5   C

Casa Rural Red NV   14.5   B

Conde de Valdemar Rioja Crianza 1996   13.5   D

Too hard for these tender lips.

**Dominio de Valdepusa Cabernet
Sauvignon, Marques de Grinon 1996**   16   E

Hugely classy beast with flavour, depth, tannins and great purpose. Brilliant bouncy fruit.

Fallers Leap Valdepusa Tempranillo 1995   13   C

Touch of cough mixture as it quits the throat.

Finca Dofi Priorat 1994   18   H

Fabulous rich and well-flavoured specimen of well-deep fruit, brisk tannins, and acidity of the class which suggests the wine will be as good but much softer in ten years. Licorice, figs, chocolate, coffee. Bottoms Up only.

Finca Valpiedra Rioja 1994 `13.5` `G`

Very expensive for what it is. Has some lush vanilla touches but it's a lot to pay for an ice cream.

Marques de Grinon Reserva Rioja 1993 `14` `E`

Navajas Rioja Crianza 1995 `15.5` `D`

Always one of the most charmingly aromatic and smoothly flavoursome of riojas.

Ochoa Tempranillo Crianza 1995 `16.5` `D`

Gorgeous ripeness, fatness, richness yet with it all there is Ochoa's great elegance, smoothness and beautiful tannic cosiness. On the delicate side for all this. Not for robust food. Lovely stuff. Bottoms Up only.

Scraping the Barrel Tempranillo NV `14` `C`

Vina Real Rioja 1994 `13.5` `D`

SPANISH WINE WHITE

Albarino Condes del Alberei 1995 `15` `D`

Campo Viejo Barrel Fermented Viura 1997 `16` `D`

What a wonderfully rich yet fresh-edged and ripe wine – polished and dry, rich and full – a great balancing act.

Casa Rural White NV `15.5` `B`

Superb value for money. Chewy, fresh, impish, delightfully clean and with a hint of exotic pineapple on the finish.

Copa Real Blanco NV `12.5` `B`

Dominio di Montalvo Rioja, Campo Viejo 1995 `10` `D`

Hate that chewy woodiness.

Euxebre Albarino Condes de Albarei 1997 `15` `D`

Creamy, hint of cauliflower, sense of salinity as an undertone – a uniquely Galician construct and it does wonders for shellfish. Wine Rack and Bottoms Up stores.

Moscatel de Valencia NV `15` `C`

Santara Viura/Chardonnay, Conca de Barbera 1996 `14` `B`

USA WINE   RED

Bonterra Cabernet Sauvignon 1996 `17` `E`

Rugged, raunchy, ripe and rivets itself to the teeth. Withal, it has some weight yet wit. Wine Rack and Bottoms Up only.

Byron Pinot Noir, Santa Barbara County 1995 `12` `G`

Columbia Crest Cote de Columbia Grenache 1995 `8` `C`

Dunnewood Dry Silk Cabernet, Seven Archers Vineyard, Alexander Valley 1994 16 F

Very classy and ripe. And indeed like crumpled silk on the tongue. Not at Thresher Wine Shops.

Dunnewood North Coast Cellars Cabernet 1995 14 D

Eagle Peak Merlot, Fetzer Vineyards 1997 16 D

Decidedly chewy yet very soft and warm. Curious paradox of styles: seems composty and ripe then goes dry and tannin-teasing, blackcurrant beneath its feet. Delicious stuff.

Fetzer Home Ranch Zinfandel 1996 15.5 D

Lovely spicy fruit here. Dry yet full of flavour and textured ripeness.

Fetzer Valley Oaks Cabernet Sauvignon 1995 14 D

Very dry.

Fetzer Valley Oaks Cabernet Sauvignon 1997 15 D

One of the most civilised, less barbarous, cabernets around.

Gallo Turning Leaf Cabernet Sauvignon 1995 15 D

Redwood Trail Pinot Noir 1997 14 D

Cherryish and not far from being an interesting pinot.

Robert Mondavi North Coast Cellars Zinfandel 1995 15 E

Robert Mondavi Oakville District Cabernet 1995   `18` `H`

A staggeringly toothsome cabernet at its peak of charm. The tobacco, the wood, the acidity, the rich fruit, the developed tannins – each works its way individually yet congeals in a huger sum of the parts. Available through Wine Rack Direct.

Robert Mondavi Reserve Pinot Noir 1995   `11` `H`

Saintsbury Pinot Noir, Carneros 1996   `12.5` `G`

Too much top on the price. Should be £4.99. Wine Rack and Bottoms Up shops only.

Sebastiani Old Vines Zinfandel, Sonoma County 1995   `14` `D`

Talus Zinfandel 1997   `14` `D`

Very juicy and rampant.

Vendange Californian Red 1998   `14` `C`

Very dry and peppery and it will perform well with rich food.

Woodbridge Mondavi Zinfandel 1996   `14` `D`

Terrific tannins here.

USA WINE   WHITE

Bonterra Chardonnay 1996   `17` `E`

Deeply serious. No joking. This is better than M. Poubelle's Montrachet. Wine Rack and Bottoms Up shops only.

Columbia Crest Chardonnay 1997 — 15.5 | D

Loads of warm, friendly fruit, humming with flavours, texture and a lush lingering strawberry/melonicity.

Fetzer Echo Ridge Sauvignon 1997 — 14 | C

Hints of a class act.

Fetzer Sundial Chardonnay, 1998 — 16 | D

Always as full of sun as the face of a California beachbum, this is fruit modelled on richness, warmth, and the flavours of the tropics. This vintage has a lovely freshness to it.

Fetzer Viognier 1998 — 16.5 | E

Lovely limpid, lush, lively – a wine of ineffable finesse yet apricot-scented and fruited richness. A rare treat. Fruit to read by, think by, listen by.

Jekel Chardonnay, Gravelstone Vineyards 1997 — 17 | E

Brilliant development: has pumpkin seeds with rich acids and plump fruit. Not as elegant as the '97 but more chutzpah! Wine Rack and Bottoms Up stores only.

Robert Mondavi Carneros Unfiltered Chardonnay 1995 — 13 | G

St Supery Sauvignon Blanc 1997 — 13 | E

Too expensive for the style.

Vendange Californian Dry White 1996 — 14 | C

Vendanges White Zinfandel 1998 — 10 | C

**Woodbridge Californian Sauvignon Blanc,
Robert Mondavi 1996**   `13` `D`

SPARKLING WINE/CHAMPAGNE

Asti Martini (Italy)   `10` `D`

Bollinger Grande Cuvee 1990   `14` `H`

Has a fat, plummy undertone. Forty-two quid? Bit rich.

Bollinger RD 1985   `13` `H`

Too dry and austere. Wine Rack and Bottoms Up only.

Bollinger Special Cuvee NV   `14` `H`

It is fine and dry.

Canard Duchene Charles VII NV   `14.5` `H`

Very good. Bottoms Up only.

Castelblanch Cava Extra Brut   `13` `C`

Charles Heidsieck 'Mis en Caves 1993' NV   `13` `H`

Charles Heidsieck 'Mis en Caves 1995' NV   `13` `H`

**Cool Ridge Sparkling Chardonnay Pinot
Noir Brut NV (Hungary)**   `12` `C`

Not as dry or as elegant as Cavas at the same price.

Deutz Marlborough Cuvee NV `13.5` `F`

Has a faintly fleshy finish.

Gosset Grande Millesime 1989 `15` `H`

Better than Krug – rather taut and fine. Bottoms Up and Wine Rack only.

Gosset Grande Reserve NV `14` `H`

Rather fine. Available in magnum size also.

Green Point Brut 1996 `15` `F`

Expensive as a cheap Champagne – but much better fruit.

Green Point Late Disgorged Brut 1992 `13` `G`

Krug Grande Cuvee NV `13` `H`

Decent enough at £20 – no more.

Krug Vintage 1989 `13.5` `H`

La Corunna Cava NV `15` `C`

Very alert bubbly of dry elegance and with a faint edge of richness. A bargain.

Lanson Vintage Gold Label 1993 `13.5` `H`

Bit light on the finish but very dry and classically tight-lipped.

Louis Roederer Brut Vintage 1993 (magnum) `13` `H`

Very warm and toasty on the finish.

Mumm Cuvee Napa Brut (California) `16` `E`

So much more assertive, refined, tasty and sanely priced than its French cousin I'm surprised there aren't serious riots in Rheims.

Mumm Cuvee Napa Rose (California) `14` `E`

Out of the Blue Lightly Sparkling (Italy) (4%) `10` `B`

Barely a wine, it might be used to seduce fleas.

Perrier-Jouet Brut Vintage 1992 `12` `H`

'PG' Pinot Grigio Frizzante `10` `C`

Piper Heidsieck Rare 1985 `17` `H`

My favourite: toast, nuts, fruit, finesse, dry, liveliness, not too old – perfect maturity. Bottoms Up only.

Pol Roger Champagne White Foil `11` `H`

Pol Roger Sir Winston Churchill Cuvee 1988 `16` `H`

Immensely proud, dry, witty, plump yet fleet of foot. Goes extremely well with cucumber sandwiches with mint. Also smoked salmon. Bottoms Up only.

Pommery Vintage 1991 `12` `H`

Not good enough. Too coarse.

Seaview Pinot Noir/Chardonnay 1994 (Australia) `16` `E`

One of Australia's strongest and tastiest challenges to Rheim's hegemony.

Seppelt Great Western Brut (Australia) 13.5 D

Veuve Clicquot La Grande Dame 1990 16 H

Rather lovely – achieves dryness yet texture and a suggestion of fruit.

UNWINS

One thing I have always enjoyed about Unwins is that the people there have a strong sense of humour. Even when I arrived at last year's Unwin wine tasting in Camden High Street and my cycle bag shot out of my hand and sent several wine bottles cascading their contents over a senior member of the wine department's suit, I was not thrown out but greeted with an understanding smile (whatever Mr Bill Rolfe, suit drenched, said in private I am pleased not to have heard). Ben Cooper, my researcher who does all the background notes for each introduction to the retailers in this book, also warmed to Unwins' sense of humour when he read that the company was offered a Comic Relief stunt which would have involved various members of the management at the chain's Dartford Kent HQ being dunked in a vat of baked beans. Ben was, so he told me, dismayed to learn that the company had pulled the plug on this idea and wondered whether the company had lost its sense of humour but I reassured him that this was not so.

Bob Maybank, PR manager for Unwins, had the difficult task of making the management's excuses for going soft on the baked beans stunt (to what end or with what motive I still haven't quite figured out) but what else are PR executives for? 'With the baked beans being very slippery, it could have been very dangerous,' he told *Off-Licence News*. Well, what about all those slippery wine writers Mr Maybank has to deal with? Lot more dangerous than a pile of harmless baked beans. My assurance of the good humour to be found at Unwins was partially restored for Ben Cooper, so he reported to me, by the photograph which accompanied this story in *Off-Licence News*.

This pictured Unwins' marketing director, the aforementioned always-a-natty-dresser Bill Rolfe, sporting a sombrero and what appeared to Ben to be a feather boa. The article went on to say that the Unwins Wine Relief initiative had raised £21,125 for Comic Relief through various activities. I felt some momentary shame at this since I turned down Jancis Robinson's request to help her raise money via Wine Relief – an initiative of her husband's – as I did not want my *Guardian* column given over to publicising inappropriate causes. I refer to the fact that Comic Relief supports Alcohol Concern, a laudable charity but not one it is surely appropriate for a red nosed wine writer to be associated with – though I endorse alcohol consumption in moderation and, for those allergic to it and liable to become dependent, abstention. In the same way, though I felt 100% sympathy for the sentiment, I did not accede to certain *Guardian* readers who wished me to boycott French wines in my column when the French held their appalling nuclear tests (and I was able to put forward reasons for this refusal which did not contradict my own boycott, years ago, of South African and Chilean wines).

Sorry to digress like this. Where was I? Oh yes, Unwins. As I have said in previous editions, Unwins enjoys a lower profile than most of its peers and the retailer seems to proceed at a gentler pace. Unwins is a family business which is still overseen by 80 family shareholders, all Wetzs (or should that be Wetzen?). The fourth generation of the Wetz family, which has run the company since the 1920s, will take the helm next year in the form of 36-year-old managing director elect, Simon Wetz. Tough name to take through school, Wetz. They must be a tough breed. (I speak with feeling on the matter of schoolboys with funny foreign names they are forced physically to stand up for.)

But the company at least had a chance to blow its own trumpet, albeit a gentle blast, when it was featured in *Off-Licence News* earlier this year. Echoing a theme from my own thoughts on Unwins in last year's guide, Mr Wetz talked about evolution rather than revolution at the company. It doesn't, Unwins' stalwart customers will be pleased to learn, sound as if the younger generation of the Wetz family is about to do anything radical. In fact, judging by what Simon Wetz says, younger members of the family are so imbued with the Unwins ethos, virtually from birth, that they seem programmed simply to continue the work of their fathers or uncles. 'We've all visited shops with our fathers when we were children, and it's very much a way of life for us,' Mr Wetz, whom I have never met, told *Off-Licence News*. He makes it sounds as if the family is a tribe of Shakers. With regard to innovation he added: 'We're looking at things all the time. It's something that the third generation was doing anyway and it's just a continuation of that.'

'It hardly sounds,' Ben Cooper retorted to me, 'like preparation for a quantum leap.' I was able to correct him. A quantum leap is exactly what it is. That is to say it is an infinitesimally small leap on the basis that a quantum (plural quanta) is merely that term in physics which refers to a sub-microscopic unit of energy sent out by or taken in by a single atom. A quantum leap, then, is surely a very small one. Sorry to lecture you, Ben, but a musical education at Cambridge obviously left a few corners brutally untutored.

But the mundane realism of Unwins (why do I always want to write Unwine? Surely this is not what dubious scientists call Freudian slippage?) takes on a certain charm when Mr Wetz discusses the idea of the family selling up. Ask this of some family-owned companies and you will get all the rhetoric about dynasties, that we are just trustees for the next generation etc. Simon Wetz puts it in rather more prosaic terms.

'You see so often family firms sell up,' he says. 'The family gets rich, spends the money in a couple of years, and then they're all stony-broke and have no jobs.' Got his feet on the ground, young Simon, and it is not, patently, just luck which has got him the job. True, he's a Wetz, but his is exactly the kind of studied sobriety required to lead a retailer like Unwine (sorry, I mean Unwins).

The *Off-Licence News* article was a chance to put the record straight but what it above all illustrated was that the popular conceptions about Unwins are most definitely founded in fact. The company moves slowly but it believes in itself and is sure that its approach is the right one for it. For instance the company has moved into Food and Wine stores and now has 18 such outlets but once again it has developed this side of the business at a snail's pace in comparison with the likes of Thresher. But current managing director Richard Rotter (his mother was called Wetz in case you're wondering and one wonders further what kind of time he had at school defending his moniker) said of this innovation: 'We are still fairly new at it. We've only had it 10 or 12 years and in our terms that's fairly short.' Yes, I was gobsmacked when I contemplated that time frame. I've been writing the *Superplonk* column for ten years now and it seems a lifetime to me. (This may suggest that Unwins inhabits some Einsteinian parallel universe, experiencing a different time and space curve than you and me, but this is not the place to speculate on such tricky matters.)

The company did of course surprise everyone with the fairly sizeable acquisition of the 72-outlet Davisons chain in 1996 but the mantle of corporate raider does not sit easily on Unwins' shoulders because it isn't one. Unwins may shortly pull another surprise because Simon Wetz is very seriously looking at the possibility of opening a store in Calais. And let's not forget that with the merger of Thresher and Victoria Wine, Unwins is now the third largest off-licence chain in the UK with a group turnover of £163.8 million. In the year 2000 it is on track to open its 400th outlet.

Unwins, I love ya. Yes, I take the piss a bit, I know. But you go into your average Unwins and you won't be greeted by a witless yob chewing gum, as I have been at other chains I won't mention. You'll be greeted by a mature human being anxious to please. Also, they like wine in spite of a name which can be so easily construed otherwise. Curiously, a love of wine is not true of every wine retailer, especially those with a brewer's skeleton at the back of the cupboard. Unwins goes its own way and they will, I have no doubt, go from strength to strength. Indeed, I made the rash forecast in a *Guardian* column some months ago that I expected them to spread north by acquiring a retailer in that neck of the woods. This was pure guesswork on my part (perhaps it was wishful thinking) and it caused a small flurry of excitement at Unwins' head office.

I shall continue to dream wild dreams on this retailer's behalf. Watch this space.

Unwins Wine Group Limited
Birchwood House
Victoria Road
Dartford
Kent DA1 5AJ
Tel: 01322 272711
Fax: 01322 294469

SEE STOP PRESS SECTION AT END OF BOOK FOR LAST-MINUTE ADDITIONS OR UPDATES TO THIS RETAILER'S RANGE.

ARGENTINIAN WINE RED

**Magdalena River Malbec/Cabernet
Sauvignon, Mendoza 1997** 13 C

Dry, reluctant to fructify.

**Magdalena River Sangiovese/Bonarda,
Mendoza 1998** 12 C

Sticky and coagulated.

Santa Julia Malbec Oak Reserve 1996 16 D

Big and ripplingly muscled. Dry yet full and deep, good
hedgerow fruitiness. Terrific energy and texture.

Santa Julia Tempranillo Oak Reserve 1997 16.5 D

Terrific soupy richness, plump dry herbiness and a finish of
tannic flourish. Great stuff.

ARGENTINIAN WINE WHITE

**Magdalena River Chardonnay, Mendoza
1997** 15 C

Very warm and richly textured (oatmeal biscuity) and the fruit
is calm, controlled and subtly fat.

215

AUSTRALIAN WINE   RED

Brown Brothers Tarrango 1997   `13.5` `D`

Grant Burge Old Vine Barossa Shiraz 1996   `13` `E`

Hill of Hope Shiraz 1997   `13.5` `D`

Sweet/sour finish.

Ironstone Shiraz/Grenache 1997   `16.5` `D`

Huge richness and bigness of fruit yet never blowsy or pretentious. Really impressive Rhone style dryness with an Italian sense of food fruitiness. Great class here.

Lindemans Bin 45 Cabernet Sauvignon 1997   `14.5` `D`

More correct than exciting but wellformed and rich to finish. Good with food.

Maglieri Shiraz, McLaren Vale 1996   `14` `E`

Mount Langi Ghiran Billi Billi Creek Shiraz/Cabernet Sauvignon 1996   `12` `E`

Parsons Brook Shiraz/Malbec 1997   `12` `D`

Bit sweet on the finish.

Penfolds Bin 35 Cabernet Sauvignon/ Shiraz/Ruby Cabernet 1997   `14` `D`

Juicy and well-meaning.

Wakefield Cabernet Sauvignon, Clare Valley 1997 `15.5` `D`

Layers of richness unfurl and they reveal raisiny ripeness, chocolate, and plums and blackberries. Solidly packed with flavour.

Wolf Blass Green Label Shiraz 1996 `14` `D`

Spicy, has bite, needs rich food (balti stuff).

Woodvale Shiraz/Cabernet 1998 `12.5` `C`

Very austere and a touch unfriendly.

AUSTRALIAN WINE WHITE

Brown Bothers Chenin Blanc 1997 `15` `C`

Delicious oriental food wine. Most individual and crisply rich.

Capel Vale CV Sauvignon Blanc/ Chardonnay 1997 `15.5` `E`

Really motors over the taste buds! Great smoked fish wine.

CV Unwooded Chardonnay, Western Australia 1997 `16.5` `E`

This is the year, '97, to wallow in the richness of the Aussie chardonnay, especially when no wood is aboard and the provenance is Western Australia. A gloriously uncluttered, elegant wine of potency, finesse and heavenly texture.

David Wynn Chardonnay, S. Australia 1997 `16` `D`

Expensive treat here. A rich, almost oily, chardonnay with a bare hint of exoticism on its finish but mostly just good, home-baked fruit.

Grant Burge Old Vine Semillon, Barossa Valley 1997 `14` `E`

Howcroft Bin 6000 Verdelho 1998 `12` `D`

Doesn't quite clinch it on the finish.

Lindemans Botrytis Riesling 1996 (half bottle) `17` `D`

Magnificently alluring bouquet suggestive of spiced soft fruit. Thereafter it's like an eccentric Trockenbeerenauslese of unusual ripeness and limpidity.

Penfolds Bin 94A Chardonnay 1994 `15` `G`

Big, rich, woody, very pretentious, creamy, Meursault-meets-Napa style, with some age ahead of it to really show its individuality. It will probably rate 17 or 17.5 in two or three years when the vegetality has undercut the smoothness of the fruit and given the wine character. At twenty pounds, it's a lot to pay and Chilean chardonnays at a quarter of the price, whilst not possessing this wine's future, do offer some competitive stylishness. At its best after dinner with goat's cheese.

Richard Hamilton Chardonnay 1996 `17` `E`

One of Australia's most determined, classy under-a-fiver chardonnays.

Tim Gramp Watervale Riesling 1997   `16.5`   `E`

Cellar it for three or four years and it'll pile on the points.

Tyrrells Long Flat Chardonnay 1998   `13.5`   `D`

Not long, but could be said to be a touch flat. Honestly labelled, at least.

Woodvale Semillon/Chardonnay 1998   `15.5`   `C`

Superb class for the money. Hints of wood, butter, and gentle melon. Well organised and stylishly fruity.

BULGARIAN WINE   RED

Cabernet Sauvignon Pulden 1997   `14.5`   `C`

Great dry richness!

Country Wine Merlot/Pinot Noir NV, Sliven   `14`   `B`

Domaine Boyar Merlot, Iambol 1997   `15`   `B`

Sweet fresh, young leather and ripe plums. Dry and stylish.

BULGARIAN WINE   WHITE

Country Wine Muskat & Ugni Blanc, Shumen NV   `14`   `B`

CHILEAN WINE RED

Canepa Zinfandel 1997 `15.5` `C`

Marzipan, cherries, and a touch of herby tannin. A real food wine, this.

Canepa Zinfandel 1998 `14` `C`

Zingy and a touch exotic, spicy and saucy. Food-slurping style and great with mild curries.

Carmen Cabernet Sauvignon 1996 `16` `C`

Delicious, savoury, ripe plums, herbs, tannins and rich acids. Great texture and tearing fruit here.

Domaine Oriental Cabernet Sauvignon 1998 `14` `D`

Warm, dry, soft and highly quaffable.

Domaine Oriental Clos Centenaire Cabernet Sauvignon 1998 `15.5` `D`

Domaine Oriental's best wine: decisive, daring, accomplished fruit with dryness, deftness and loads of style. Rather classy to finish.

Domaine Oriental Clos Centenaire Merlot, Maule Valley 1997 `14` `D`

Errazuriz Cabernet Sauvignon 1997 `16` `D`

Has that wonderful wildness of heart! Great savoury finish.

Errazuriz Sena 1995 `13` `H`

Compelling texture and richness – almost Port-like – but the price? Absurd!

Errazuriz Syrah Reserve, Aconcagua 1997 `17.5` `E`

Big, berried fruit, rugged yet immensely soft, huge depth, flavour and commanding richness. This is even better than it was in the summer of '98 when I first tasted it.

Gracia Cabernet Sauvignon 1995 `15.5` `E`

Beats at the Aussie door and is not far from knocking it down.

Gracia Merlot Reserve, Aconcagua 1997 `16.5` `E`

Huge depth of flavour here, leather/blackcurrant/plum, and great developed tannins. Brilliant tone, polish, character and style.

La Palmeria Merlot 1998 `16.5` `C`

It combines that wonderful Chilean double-whammy of food fitness and great, concentrated, complex drinking. Gorgeous stuff.

CHILEAN WINE WHITE

Casablanca Chardonnay 1998 `15.5` `D`

Delicious smokey richness and lithe acidity combine winningly.

Domaine Oriental Chardonnay 1998 `13.5` `C`

Domaine Oriental Clos Centenaire Chardonnay 1998

Very floppy on the finish, lazy wine.

Domaine Oriental Sauvignon Blanc, Maule Valley 1998

`13.5` `C`

Errazuriz Wild Ferment Chardonnay, Casablanca 1997

`16.5` `E`

Wonderful that the wine should wish to keep its only synthetic touch as its cork, thus preserving from natural cork taint the delicate, natural fruitiness of what is a lovely, understated wine. Many Chilean chardonnays at half the price of this one are fruitier but this is not about sheer fruit. This wine is about texture, very subtle complexity and flavours you have to search for.

Gracia Chardonnay Reserve, Cachapoal 1997

La Palmeria Chardonnay 1998

`15` `C`

Restrained, rich, charming acidity, subtle lemon flavours.

ENGLISH WINE   WHITE

Lamberhurst Bacchus 1996

Tries hard, but a touch prissy.

222

FRENCH WINE RED

Ash Ridge Grenache/Merlot 1998 `13.5` `C`

Bit squashy, as if bruised fruit were used. Has some lively tannins, though.

Ash Ridge Merlot d'Oc 1997 `14` `C`

Ash Ridge Syrah d'Oc 1998 `13.5` `C`

Starts fruity and alert and youthful but ends wrinkled and geriatric.

Beaujolais Georges Duboeuf 1997 `10` `D`

Oh, come on Georges.

Bourgogne Hautes Cotes de Nuits 1995 `10` `E`

Begins in a reasonable pinot fashion, aromatically, then rapidly descends into anonymous, anodyne sweetness. A swindle, fruit like this.

Cabardes Chateau Ventenac, Alain Maurel 1997 `15` `C`

Lingering richness and eventual dryness here. Good with casseroles.

Cabrieres Coteaux du Languedoc 1996 `13` `C`

Finishes a bit early at the back of the palate before it reaches the parched throat.

Chassagne Montrachet Louis Jadot 1994 `11` `G`

Chateau Astruc Minervois 1998   14.5   C

Lovely layers of warm fruit which continue to surge softly and savourily all the way down.

Chateau Bellevue la Foret Cotes du Frontonnais 1996   12   C

Chateau Beychevelle St Julien 4eme Cru 1995   12   H

Something here.

Chateau Croizet-Bages Pauillac 5eme Cru 1995   11   H

Soapy.

Chateau de la Roulerie, Les Maronis Anjou Rouge 1997   16   D

Superb cabernet franc savouriness, wild raspberry-and-bitter-cherry fruit and a great stomping finish. Great for mood and food.

Chateau Giscours Margaux 3eme Cru 1995   11   H

Chateau Lascombes, Margaux 2eme Cru 1995   10   H

Chateau le Raz Cotes de Bergerac 1996   15.5   D

Wonderful herby dryness and bigness of flavour. A generous, firmly textured wine of humour and warmth.

Chateau Pavie St Emilion Grand Cru 'B' 1995   11   H

Raw.

Claret Special Reserve Yvon Mau 1996 `13` `C`

Cuvee Philippe VdP Herault 1998 `13` `B`

Dry, earthy, thin, cherry-fruited. Can be chilled and drunk with fish but it is essentially a party wine to raise funds for New Labour.

Domaine de la Grand Bellane, Valreas 1997 `16` `D`

Ragged yet dainty on its feet, this richly finishing, very dry wine combines a fair spread of hedgerow fruit and delicious tannin. It is classic Rhone Villages red. Great drunk out of a Viking horn or sipped with *lievre a la royale*.

Domaine de la Soleiade, Vacqueyras 1998 `15` `D`

Soft, bruised-fruit texture, hint of thyme and a big fruity finish. Highly drinkable.

Domaine du Cler de Tart Premier Cru, Morey St Denis La Forge 1994 `10` `G`

Faugeres Domaine d'Azil 1997 `16` `C`

Real character, warmth, herbiness, dryness and savoury depth here. Great value tannins, worth the price of admission alone.

Fitou Chateau de Segure 1996 `14` `D`

Very bright, yet finishes dry. Needs food and company.

Fleur de Bryuere VdP du Torgan 1998 `12` `B`

So light you can read a book through it.

Graves Oak Aged, Yvon Mau 1997 `14.5` `D`

Good claret style: dryness and richness here. Most engaging (but very dry).

Hautes Cotes de Nuits Tastevinage 1995 · 13 · E

James Herrick Cuvee Simone 1997 · 16.5 · C

Gorgeous, tobacco and plum aroma, invigoratingly rich, dry fruit as the palate is struck, and a fine fulfilling finish. Classy and full of wit, this wine. Fantastic price, too.

La Ciboise Coteaux du Tricastin 1997 · 13.5 · D

Oddly constrained finish.

La Cigaliere Cotes du Rhone 1998 · 15 · C

Nice herby plums here, fresh and eager, and a good clump of baked earth on the finish.

Les Beaux Sites Domaine de Castan Cabernet Sauvignon 1997 · 15.5 · C

Delicious tannins, exciting mature fruit (oily, ripe), hint of flowers, but overall it's the Midi scrub which predominates.

Lirac Domaine Duseigneur 1996 · 13 · D

Madiran Chateau de Crouseilles 1993 · 14 · E

Getting a bit dried out, and the fruit pruney and crotchety. But with a spicy dish, it would explode with flavour.

Marsannay Rouge Louis Jadot 1996 · 10 · F

Morgon 'Cave Bocabarteille' 1997 · 10 · D

Pinot Noir Reserve Personnelle 1995 · 12 · E

FRENCH WINE WHITE

Anjou Blanc 1997 `11` `C`

Bit sweet for me.

Ash Ridge Sauvignon Blanc VdP d'Oc 1997 `12.5` `C`

Bergerac Comtesse Catherine 1997 `13` `B`

Cabernet d'Anjou, Celliers du Prieure 1998 `10` `C`

Sweet and uneven.

**Chateau Mire l'Etang, Coteaux du
Languedoc La Clape 1997 (oaked)** `12` `C`

Corbieres Les Producteurs du Mont Tauch `12` `C`

Cuvee Philippe VdP Comte Tolosan 1998 `14.5` `B`

Simply delicious and lemon tinged. Great quaffing and fish
wine.

**Domaine de Saubagnere Cotes de
Gascogne 1998** `14` `C`

Not as exotic as some specimens of this breed, but still nicely
pineappley and all-singingly fresh and cheeky.

**Gewurztraminer Grand Cru Pfersigberg,
Cuvee Jeremy 1989 (half bottle)** `16.5` `G`

A wonderful half bottle for a special event. Creme brulee and
lemon butterscotch fruit – marvellous!

Graves Oak Aged, Yvon Mau 1998 13 D

Good oyster wine, but a touch pricey.

Les Trois Herault Les Chais Beaucarois NV 13 B

Macon Lugny Les Charmes 1997 15 D

One of the tastiest minor white burgundies about. Classic vegetality and dryness of unpretentious demeanour and style.

Muscadet de Sevres et Maine l'Herminiere 1998 12 C

Muscadet sur Lie Pierre Brevin 1997 13.5 C

Petit Chablis Albert Bichot 1998 11 D

Ludicrously under-engineered and overpriced fruit.

Puligny Montrachet Louis Jadot 1996 12 G

Too much money by far.

Sancerre Jean Sablenay 1997 12 E

Tokay Pinot Gris Kuentz-Bas 1996 16 E

Lovely apricot/pineapple/lemon fruit which is subtle yet striking.

GERMAN WINE WHITE

Fitz Ritter Durkheimer Hochbenn Riesling Kabinett 1997 10 D

Struggles.

GREEK WINE   RED

Retsina of Attica 'Kourtaki'   `13` `B`

HUNGARIAN WINE   RED

**Blue Remembered Hills Blauer Zweigelt
1997**   `12` `C`

Volcanic Hills Kekfrancos 1997   `13` `C`

HUNGARIAN WINE   WHITE

Chapel Hill Irsai Oliver, Balatonboglar 1997   `13.5` `B`

**Chapel Hill Oaked Chardonnay,
Balatonboglar 1997**   `13` `C`

ITALIAN WINE   RED

Chianti Villa Selva 1997   `12` `C`

Bit dull for a fiver, juicy.

ITALIAN RED

Ciro Classico Librandi 1997 `14` `C`

Needs rich food. It's so advanced and mature. The fruit is raisiny
and superripe. Try chicken dhansak.

Montepulciano d'Abruzzo, Miglianico 1997 `15.5` `C`

Scrumptious fruit here: spicy yet dry, fruity yet firm – deliciously
well formed from tongue tip to larynx.

Sangiovese di Puglia, Vigneti di Sole 1997 `13` `C`

Terre di Realdore 'Le Monferine' Barbera d'Asti 1997 `16` `C`

Terrific pacey richness and ripeness here: touch of spice, violets,
meaty richness and a fine dry finish of some aplomb.

ITALIAN WINE WHITE

Alasia Chardonnay del Piemonte 1998 `13.5` `C`

Fontana Morella Cerveteri 1997 `11` `C`

La Mura Bianco, Bombina 1998 `14` `C`

Curiously fatty fruit, hardly a hint of floral freshness, but has
some regional rustic charm.

NEW ZEALAND WINE RED

Delegat's Hawkes Bay Cabernet Sauvignon/Merlot 1996 `13` `D`

Sacred Hill Basket Press Merlot/Cabernet, Hawkes Bay 1995 `13.5` `E`

Waimanu 1996 `13` `C`

Tastes like a whacky pinot noir.

NEW ZEALAND WINE WHITE

Corbans Gisborne Chardonnay 1997 `13` `D`

Bit of a disappointing finish.

Lawson's Dry Hills Chardonnay 1997 `12.5` `E`

Already showing its age – incredible colour development and caramel undertone (the equivalent of wrinkles where chardonnay is concerned).

Linden Estate Sauvignon Blanc 1997 `13.5` `D`

Almost . . .

Marlborough Gold Sauvignon Blanc 1998 `13` `C`

Bit flighty for a Kiwi.

Oyster Bay Chardonnay, Marlborough 1998 `16` `D`

Delicate, decisive, delicious, utterly quaffable – has finesse, flavour and is not remotely flash.

Oyster Bay Sauvignon Blanc 1998 `16` `D`

Quite lively richness yet restrained fluency of rippling fruit.

**Sacred Hill Barrique Fermented
Chardonnay 1996** 15.5 E

**Seifried Estate Sauvignon Blanc, Nelson
1998** 11 D

**Waimanu Muller-Thurgau & Sauvignon
Blanc 1998** 14 C

Getting better, this wine, with this vintage. More defined and refined.

PORTUGUESE WINE RED

Bela Fonte Baga 1997 15.5 C

Terrific juicy fruit here. Delicious tarry richness and mature juiciness.

Bela Fonte Jaen 1998 16 C

Pruney and polished, stickily textured and full of vim and verve. Great gobbets of shapely fruit excite the taste buds.

Dao Dom Ferraz 1997 16.5 C

Fabulous tufted texture and soft, ripe, curvaceous fruit. It really wraps itself round the taste buds. Quite gorgeously quaffable and delicious.

Douro Vega 1997 14 C

At its ripely perfect peak of gluggability.

Pedras do Monte Castelao 1998 `16` `C`

Energy, youth, soft thickness of savoury fruit overlaid by fleshy plums. Superb individuality.

Portada Vinho Regional Estremadura 1996 `15` `C`

Layers of fresh jam interleafed with tannins and pert acidity. Integrated, fresh, firm – a lot going for it.

**Quinta das Setencostas, Alenquer
Region 1997** `14` `C`

Segada Baga/Trincadeira, Ribatejo 1997 `13.5` `C`

Sweet and ripe, but has some back-up tannins which take time to become full-frontal. Needs food, this wine.

PORTUGUESE WINE WHITE

Bical Bela Fonte 1997 `15` `C`

Segada Fernao Pires, Ribatejo 1998 `16` `C`

Lovely texture and polish to this distinctly individual and delicious wine. Utterly compellingly quaffable and thought-provoking.

SOUTH AFRICAN WINE RED

Beyerskloof Pinotage, Stellenbosch 1997 `14` `D`

Cape Cinsault/Merlot 1998 `14` `C`

Good ripeness without OTTness here. Plummy, fruity/dry, good texture and balance, warm finish.

Cape Red 1998 `13.5` `C`

Sticky and warm. Needs air conditioning.

Clos Malverne Cabernet/Shiraz, Stellenbosch 1997 `14.5` `D`

Spicy, rich, hedgerow-fruity and thick, this is a good wine for elegant Indian dishes. Has come on wonderfully in bottle since I tasted it last year.

Clos Malverne Pinotage, Stellenbosch 1997 `16` `D`

Wonderful! Tobacco, black cherries and tannin.

Glen Carlou Merlot, Paarl 1997 `13` `E`

Leef Op Hoop Cabernet Sauvignon/Merlot, Stellenbosch 1996 `13` `D`

Neil Joubert Cabernet Sauvignon 1997 `13` `D`

Bit juicy for this old palate.

SOUTH AFRICAN WINE WHITE

Boschendal Sauvignon Blanc, Paarl 1996 `13` `D`

Cape Chardonnay, Stellenbosch 1998 `13.5` `C`

Odd cosmetic tang.

Cape White 1998

Touch dull.

Fairview Chardonnay 1998

The best chardonnay for the money at Unwins? Could be. The richness and class are superb.

Jordan Chardonnay, Stellenbosch 1997 15 E

Big chewy white burgundy taste-alike. Great wine for chicken and posh sea-food dishes.

SPANISH WINE   RED

Conde de Valdemar Reserva 1994

Creamy vanilla fruit which is very expensive but with a great Indian dish, meaty and proud, this would be wonderful.

Cosme Palacio y Hermanos Rioja 1996

Drying out a touch and getting a little grouchy.

Don Darias NV

Terrific new-found polish and plumpness.

Ochoa Tempranillo Crianza 1996 13 D

Bit over the hill now. But good with Indian food (the raisiny fruit melds with the spices).

Senorio de Nava Ribera del Duero 1997

Touch expensive for the dryness of the fruit. Seems old, too, this specimen.

Tapon de Oro Garnacha 1998 `12.5` `D`

Ripe and a touch sweet.

Vinas del Vero Cabernet Sauvignon 1997 `14` `D`

Comes good on the finish after an uncertain start.

Vinas del Vero Gran Vos Reserva 1995 `14` `E`

Very dry, it seems, but reaches beyond itself to provide a startling finish of berries and rich tannins. An expensive treat to go with Christmas fowls.

SPANISH WINE WHITE

Ochoa Rosada Garnacha 1998 `14` `D`

A stern, dry rosé which throws in a bright cherry and cheery finish.

Vinas del Vero Chardonnay 1998 `14.5` `C`

Has some flavour, bite and, though subdued, personality.

Vinas del Vero Clarion, Somontano 1997 `13` `E`

Too expensive to rate higher. Thinks too much of itself, this wine.

USA WINE RED

Beringer Zinfandel, California 1995 `14` `D`

Blossom Hill NV

Horrible sweet, marzipan-tinged fruit.

De Loach Zinfandel Platinum 1996

Almost good but the finish gets toffeed and sweet.

Easton Zinfandel, Shenandoah Valley 1995

Fetzer Valley Oaks Cabernet Sauvignon, California 1995

Very dry.

USA WINE WHITE

Beringer Sauvignon Blanc, California 1996

Lovely smokey edge to some rich, concentrated fruit. Classy, vigorous, bold.

Blossom Hill NV

So unremarkable it's staggering grapes bothered to get crushed for it.

Byron Chardonnay, Santa Barbara 1994 13 G

Fetzer Viognier 1998 16.5 E

Lovely limpid, lush, lively – a wine of ineffable finesse yet apricot-scented and fruited richness. A rare treat. Fruit to read by, think by, listen by.

237

Sutter Home Chardonnay 1997

Under-a-fiver Cal chardonnay? When it's good, it's creamy and rich and great with food.

Sutter Home White Zinfandel 1998

An abomination. Zinfandel is a red wine not a sweet pink gunge. An act of criminality.

Wente Chardonnay, California 1996

FORTIFIED WINE

Calem 10 Year Old Port

Calem Late Bottled Vintage Port 1994

Superb value. As good as many vintage ports: languorous, rich, pruney, ripe, textured and piles of thick, sweet fruit which is never monodimensional.

Calem Quinta da Foz Port 1987

Touch expensive for the sweetness of the finish.

Dom Ramos Manzanilla

Dos Cortados Dry Old Oloroso Sherry

Matusalem Sweet Old Oloroso Sherry

SPARKLING WINE/CHAMPAGNE

Chardonnay Blanc de Blancs 'Le Baron' Brut
`13.5` `D`

Conniston Stockmans Bridge NV (Australia)
`13` `D`

Bit obvious.

Duchatel Brut Champagne NV
`13` `F`

Bit austere and simplistic for thirteen pounds.

Duchatel Vintage Champagne 1994
`12` `G`

Bit austere and simplistic for thirteen pounds. Don't go overboard on the flavour.

Freixenet Cava Brut NV
`15.5` `D`

Lovely soft richness, restrained and classy. Such a satisfying construct under £5.50.

Graham Beck Brut NV (South Africa)
`14` `D`

Crisp and gently fruity.

Jacob's Creek Sparkling Chardonnay/Pinot Noir NV (Australia)
`15` `D`

Great value.

Lindauer Brut NV (New Zealand)
`14.5` `E`

Expressive of nothing but great value for money and utterly charming sipping.

Nicolas Feuillate Brut Premier Cru NV `14` `G`

Seaview Brut Rose `15` `D`

Stockman's Bridge Brut (Australia) `12` `D`

VICTORIA WINE

Please refer to First Quench introduction on page 169.

ARGENTINIAN WINE WHITE

Correas Torrontes/Chardonnay 1997 `10` `C`

So cosmetic!

Norton Torrontes, Mendoza 1999 `13` `C`

Santa Julia Chardonnay 1998 `14` `C`

AUSTRALIAN WINE RED

Leasingham Grenache 1996 `15.5` `E`

This is improving nicely in bottle. Terrific sweet/rich, soft/hard, juicy/dry grenache.

Nanya Estate Malbec/Ruby Cabernet 1998 `14.5` `C`

Almonds, plums, and a baked soft-fruit edge make this a plump specimen, food-friendly and mood-friendly.

Oxford Landing Merlot 1998 `14.5` `D`

A solid merlot rather than a thrilling one, it has some charm and propriety, manners and merlot credentials.

Saltram Shiraz 1996 `13` `D`

Samuels Bay Grenache 1997 `16` `D`

One of the most concentrated grenaches I've tasted. Plummy,

cigar-edged, perfumed, rich, very free-flowing yet delicate, this
is an immensely quaffable food wine of considerable charm.

Samuels Bay Malbec, Padthaway 1995   15   D

Soupy and juicy and great with Indian food. Selected stores.

Shirazamatazz 1996   15   D

St Hallett Barossa Shiraz 1997   13   E

Too juicy for eight quid.

Tatachilla Grenache Shiraz 1998   16   D

This estate has come on so much since it changed ownership.
A decade ago I saw grapes destined for Tatachilla swollen with
irrigated water but not the beauties which went into this bargain
blend. The wine has style, bravura, loads of fruit but is never
silly or too juicy. The tannins are temperate and tasty. With
increasing Oz prices, this is a sane specimen in a mad world.

Wynn's Coonawarra Shiraz 1996   16.5   D

Superbly classy and rich. Hints of mint cling to the deeply
textured (denim and corduroy) fruit (plums, cherries and blackcurrants) and the sheer cheek of the fruit, its bounce yet gravitas,
is terrific – the finish is syrup of figs. Martha's Vineyard only.

AUSTRALIAN WINE   WHITE

Black Noble de Bortolia NV (half bottle)   16   F

Cough mixture meets old, molasses-rich sherry. A remarkably

thick pudding wine to handsomely partner Christmas pudding or to pour over ice cream. It would be a superb accompaniment to *tarte tatin*.

David Traeger Verdelho, Victoria 1998

A real spicy treat! Lovely pineapple/citrus edging to ripe peach and pear fruit. Great quaffing and oriental food wine. Selected stores.

Koala Falls Chardonnay/Semillon 1997

Lindemans Bin 70 Semillon/Verdelho/ Sauvignon Blanc/Chardonnay 1997

Lindemans Botrytis Riesling 1996 (half bottle)

Magnificently alluring bouquet suggestive of spiced soft fruit. Thereafter it's like an eccentric Trockenbeerenauslese of unusual ripeness and limpidity.

Mitchelton Chardonnay 1996

Oxford Landing Sauvignon Blanc 1999

Very fresh and perky. Good finish to an elegant wine.

Pewsey Vale Riesling 1997

The satin texture is one thing, the nigh-classic aroma is another (something no European riesling acquires so young), and the finish is yet another. Even so, you can cellar it for five more years and who knows if perfection won't emerge?

Thomas Mitchell Marsanne 1996

Terrific oily fruit of substance, wit and staying power. Supreme idea to match with Thai fishcakes, scallops, squid etc.

Tollana Unoaked Chardonnay 1999 `15.5` `C`

More attentive to the purity of chardonnay fruit, unmasked by wood, than a million Chablis at three times the price. New World richness, yes, but it's subtle.

BULGARIAN WINE RED

Copper Crossing Red NV `14` `B`

Simple fruity quaffing. Good with food, too. Has a dry edge.

Domaine Boyar Premium Oaked Cabernet Shumen 1997 `13.5` `C`

Domaine Boyar Premium Reserve Cabernet Sauvignon 1996 `14` `C`

Very approachable.

Domaine Boyar Premium Reserve Merlot 1996 `14` `C`

Hints of leather and a subtle spiciness.

Premier Oaked Cabernet Sauvignon 1997 `13.5` `C`

Premier Oaked Merlot 1997 `14.5` `C`

Touch more meat, aroma and tannin in the oaked version. A good casserole wine.

Premier Reserve Cabernet Sauvignon 1996 `14.5` `C`

An approachable level of rich, soft fruit which strikes a handsome dry note as it quits the throat.

Premier Reserve Merlot 1996

Touch fruity on the finish but some worthy fruit on the middle of the palate and a pleasing perfume.

Stowells Bulgarian Red (3-litre box)

Price band is the equivalent for 75cl.

BULGARIAN WINE WHITE

Boyar Muskat & Ugni Blanc NV

Copper Crossing Dry White NV

Lovely glugging fruit here: crisp, clean, medium-bodied fruit of great charm.

Domaine de Boyar Targovischte Chardonnay 1997

More like a sauvignon than anything.

CHILEAN WINE RED

Cono Sur Cabernet Sauvignon, Rapel 1998

Unusually gruff-voiced, gravely Chilean cabernet – but high class and very accomplished.

Cono Sur Pinot Noir 1998

Plastic corked and otherwise not typical pinot either. It has some rich tannins for a start and the cherry undertone has to be searched for. But, as a solid red, it's absolutely fine.

La Palmeria Cabernet/Merlot 1997

So compellingly complex and gluggable you scrutinise the price tag with as much astonishment as you behold the wonderful fruit. Selected stores.

La Palmeria Cabernet/Merlot 1998

Very dark and savoury. A big-shouldered wine which pulls its weight with food.

Las Colinas Cabernet 1998

Dry, vegetal, touch stalky and typically rich on the throat.

Valdivieso Malbec 1998

Malbec as smooth and plump as it comes picked.

CHILEAN WINE WHITE

Concha y Toro Casillero del Diablo Chardonnay 1997

Not as gracious as previous vintages, but still a fair chardonnay under a fiver.

Cono Sur Gewurztraminer 1997

Bit florid and blowsy.

La Palmeria Chardonnay 1998 `15` `C`

Restrained, rich, charming acidity, subtle lemon/lemon flavours.

Las Colinas Sauvignon Blanc 1998 `14` `C`

Hint of grass tickles the nose, then gets richer and fatter as the fruit meets the palate.

ENGLISH WINE WHITE

Summerhill Dry White `11` `C`

FRENCH WINE RED

Abbotts Cumulus Shiraz Minervois 1998 `15` `D`

The polish to the herbs and Midi-mannered earthiness is terrific.

Beaujolais AC Regional Classics 1997 `13.5` `C`

The label speaks true: a soft fruity red. No mention, though, of the palate's discovery of a pleasant dry cherry finish.

Beaujolais Villages Duboeuf 1997 `13` `D`

Pushy name, not so pushy fruit, adventurous price.

**Charles de France Bourgogne Pinot
Noir 1996** `11` `D`

Chateau Beauvoisin, Costieres de Nimes 1995   16   C

Real swashbuckling richness, flavour, individuality and style here. Great balance of elements with fruit emerging the flavoursome winner over tannins and acidity. Wine Cellars and Martha's Vineyard only.

Chateau d'Aiguilhe, Cotes de Castillon 1994   15   E

A fat mouthful with a rascally finish and edge of mannered leatheriness and good tannins. Wine Rack and Bottoms Up only.

Chateau Langoiran Cuvee Classique 1996   13.5   E

Juicy (unusually so for a Cotes de Bordeaux) – but it does go dry-as-dust on the finish.

Chateau Sauvage Premier Cotes de Bordeaux 1997   15   D

Excellent claret here where the bristly tannins are controlled by textured classy fruit.

Chateau Suau, 1er Cotes de Bordeaux 1997 (unoaked)   13.5   D

Very firm and fruity, not remotely like claret – it's quaffable.

Cornas Les Nobles Rives, Cotes de Tain 1994   14   F

Cote Rotie, Domaine de Bonserine 1996   10   H

Cotes de Beaune Villages 1996   12   E

Strains to portray itself as wine rather than fruit juice.

Cotes du Rhone 1997 `13` `C`

Cotes du Rhone Chateau du Grand Prebois 1995 `14` `D`

Lot of well-cooked meat here.

Cotes du Rhone Villages Les Faisans 1998 `14` `C`

Very smooth, unhurried, calm and fruity performer. Not a dry eye in the house.

Cotes du Ventoux La Mission 1997 `14` `C`

Good herby fruit with a touch of the sun.

Dark Horse Cahors 1998 `14` `C`

An attempt to civilise the black wine of Cahors.

Fitou Special Reserve 1997 `14.5` `C`

Ripe yet dry. Good chilled. Selected stores.

Fleurie Georges Duboeuf 1998 `11` `E`

Selected stores.

Fleurie Regional Classics 1998 `13.5` `D`

Very juicy and drinkable with a hint of character – but seven quid? That takes some swallowing.

French Connection Cabernet/Syrah 1998 `14` `C`

Juicy but dry to finish.

French Full Red VdP d'Oc NV, Victoria Wine `13` `B`

Grenache VdP des Coteaux de l'Ardeche 1997 `14.5` `B`

Mont Tauch Old Bush Vines Carignan 1998 `13` `C`

Very juicy.

Pommard, Domaine du Fief de Montjeu 1996 `10` `G`

Red Burgundy Vergy 1997 `12` `C`

Fruit juice.

Roc Saint Vincent Bordeaux 1997 `13` `C`

Saumur Joseph Verdier 1997 `14.5` `C`

Stowells of Chelsea Merlot VdP d'Oc (3-litre box) `14` `C`

Price band is the equivalent for 75cl.

Stowells Vin de Pays du Gard (3-litre box) `13.5` `B`

Price band is the equivalent for 75cl.

FRENCH WINE   WHITE

Bordeaux Blanc 1997 `13` `B`

Bordeaux Sauvignon Calvet 1997 `12` `C`

Chablis Regional Classics 1997 `12.5` `E`

Not eight quid's worth of fruit, I feel.

Chablis Vieilles Vignes, Defaix 1996 · 11 · F

Eleven pounds? Pull the other one.

Chablis Vieilles Vignes, La Cuvee Exceptionelle, Defaix 1997 · 12.5 · G

Seventeen pounds! Incredible.

Chateau Bonnet Entre Deux Mers 1998 · 12 · D

Touch muddled.

Chateau Bonnet Oak Aged Entre Deux Mers 1996 · 13 · E

Too much wood for the paucity of fruit.

Chateau de Tariquet Chardonnay 1998 · 14 · D

A posh version of Cotes de Gascogne.

Chateau Filhot Sauternes 1990 · 15 · H

Lovely burnt butter, honey, nuts and creme brulee fruit. A pudding wine of elegance and distinction.

Chateau La Tuque Bordeaux 1997 · 14.5 · C

Chateau Petit Moulin Blanc, Bordeaux 1998 · 12.5 · D

A little less muddled that Chateau Bonnet.

Colombard Sauvignon Blanc au Loubet Vignoble Gascogne 1998 · 13.5 · C

Crisp and appley.

FRENCH WHITE

French Dry VdP d'Oc, Victoria Wine `13.5` `B`

French Medium VdP d'Oc, Victoria Wine `13.5` `B`

James Herrick Chardonnay VdP d'Oc 1998 `16.5` `C`

Such delicacy of richness and toasty, nutty finish. Quite deliciously daring! Selected stores.

Laperriere Chardonnay VdP du Jardin de la France 1997 `14.5` `C`

Le Vieux Mas Marsanne Viognier VdP d'Oc 1998 `15` `C`

Dry with a hint of minerals and fruit. Good smoked fish wine.

Meursault, Les Chevaliers, Domaine Rene Monnier 1996 `12` `G`

Montagny Premier Cru Oak Aged Chardonnay 1997 `13.5` `D`

Muscadet Cotes de Grandlieu 1998 `13` `C`

Be okay with oysters.

Muscadet de Sevre et Maine Sur Lie, Domaine de la Roulerie 1997 `12` `C`

Rivers Meet White Bordeaux 1997 `11` `C`

Bit dullish. Selected stores.

Stowells of Chelsea VdP du Tarn (3-litre box) `14` `B`

Price band is the equivalent for 75cl.

Tequirat Cotes de Gascogne 1998　　14　C

Exotic touches to this fresh, fruity, impishly refreshing wine.

**The French Connection Chardonnay/
Viognier VdP d'Oc 1997**　　15　C

Tokay Pinot Gris, Cave de Turckheim 1997　　13.5　D

Tokay Pinot Gris, Turckheim 1998　　13.5　D

Needs another eighteen months to rouse the apricots in the bottle and raise the rating to 16.5 points.

Turckheim Gewurztraminer 1998　　16　D

Classic, spicy, rich, warm, immediate rosy/lychee/strawberry fruit. Great throat refresher and plate accompanist.

Turckheim Pinot Blanc 1998　　14.5　C

I love the texture of this ripe, appley/pear (subtle touches, these), richly intentioned wine. It's an individual wine of character.

GERMAN WINE　　WHITE

Kendermann Dry Riesling 1998　　12.5　C

This even dares to say 'Vineyard Selection' on the label, as though this coveys anything unusual. Where do they imagine we think the grapes come from? The greengrocer's? Well, come to think of it . . .

HUNGARIAN WINE   WHITE

AK 28 Sauvignon Blanc 1998   13 | C

Curious squashed fruit finish from an austere-seeming overtone aromatically.

AK 68 Pink Pinot Gris 1998   11 | C

Odd and oddly unsatisfactory on the finish.

Hilltop Gewurztraminer Slow Fermented 1997   12 | C

The '98 will be much better!

ITALIAN WINE   RED

Cecchi Sangiovese 1998   14.5 | C

Meatier, brisker, fruitier and altogether more charming than many a Chianti.

Chianti Classico Rocca di Castignoli 1996   13.5 | D

Salice Salento Vallone 1996   14 | C

Totally prepared for food.

Trulli Negroamaro 1997   14.5 | C

Warm, savoury, very polished and almost sedate in its mouthful, it packs a punch of gentility, yet style. Hint of leather to it.

Trulli Primitivo 1997

Spicy, warm, herbal, rich, yet has a stealth-of-foot deftness as it quits the throat. Generous quaffing here and food-friendliness.

Zagara Sangiovese Syrah 1997

Chianti meets the Clare Valley in this Sicilian production of jammy ripeness.

ITALIAN WINE WHITE

Falerio Pilastri Saladini 1998

Has the nervous finish of Italian fish wine.

Trulli Chardonnay Salento 1998

Delicate progression of richness yet delicacy courses over the taste buds here, leaving one refreshed and panting for more. It would be easy to quaff this wine too quickly and miss its abundant charms as it trips, with variegated steps, down the throat.

Trulli Dry Muscat 1998

Lovely floral edge, dry as you like it, and not a sissy side in sight. A sophisticated aperitif or to go with minted fish dishes and tomato tarts.

Verdicchio dei Castelli di Jesi Verbacco 1998

Nicely crisp but with an underlying fruity flow.

MEXICAN WINE RED

Casa Madero Cabernet Sauvignon 1997   `13.5` `D`

MEXICAN WINE WHITE

Casa Madero Chardonnay 1997   `13.5` `C`

NEW ZEALAND WINE RED

Church Road Cabernet Sauvignon/Merlot 1997   `14` `E`

Bit expensive for admittedly drinkable fruit – nine quid gives you something to think about. Selected stores.

Montana Reserve Merlot 1997   `14` `E`

Expensive but a very good stab at a reserve merlot – aroma, leather, touch of spice, good texture and some satisfying length on the finish. Nine quid, though? Well . . .

NEW ZEALAND WINE WHITE

Azure Bay Chardonnay/Semillon 1998   `14` `C`

Great with a Chinese takeaway.

Church Road Chardonnay 1998   16   E

Gorgeous price, true, but then so is the fruit. It has great smoky flavour and texture.

Cooks Gisborne Chardonnay 1997   13   D

Dashwood Sauvignon Blanc, Marlborough
1997   15.5   D

Dry honey, gooseberry jam – luscious and rather ornate.

Montana Reserve Chardonnay 1998   15   E

Nothing reserved about the fruit as it hits the palate. Not elegant but magically entertaining.

Montana Reserve Gewurztraminer 1998   15   E

Melon, peaches and raspberries – delicious.

Villa Maria Private Bin Chardonnay,
Marlborough 1997   14   D

Villa Maria Private Bin Sauvignon,
Marlborough 1998   14.5   D

Quiet, reserved and very dainty. A thought provocative wine which needs no food.

Villa Maria Riesling 1998   15.5   D

Lovely now but in two or three years? Maybe 17 or 18 points. Terrific lilting fruit on the finish.

PORTUGUESE WINE RED

Bright Brothers Douro Red 1996

Finishes a touch juicily for a fiver.

Dom Ferraz Dao 1997

Fabulous tufted texture and soft, ripe, curvaceous fruit. It really wraps itself round the taste buds. Quite gorgeously quaffable and delicious.

Fiuza Cabernet Sauvignon 1997

Chilled, great with fish. Warmer, great with meat and veg. In a glass, amusing to contemplate. On the palate, fresh and plummy and enjoyable.

Pedras do Monte 1998

From the terrific '98 vintage, this superb example of rich, balanced fruit offers bargain drinking. The tannins are decent yet very soft, savoury and smooth.

Ramada Red 1998

Juicier than previous vintages. Odd, considering how rich the '98 vintage in Portugal was.

Terra Boa Tras o Montes 1998

Tannins get going eventually alongside some warm, rich fruit. has some character to it, this wine.

Terra Boa Vinho Tinto 1997

Selected stores.

ROMANIAN WINE RED

River Route Limited Edition Merlot 1996

Cherries, hint of leather, savoury finish. Great glugging here.

River Route Pinot Noir 1998

More pinot-like in perfume and in its lush, feral aftertaste than many a Cotes de Beaune at three times the price.

SOUTH AFRICAN WINE RED

Boland Wynkelder Merlot/Shiraz 1997

Cape View Cinsaut/Shiraz 1998

Hmm . . . Took some getting, that 14 points. At £4.49 the wine is pricey. However, it's honest, dry, cherry-ripe and quaffable. But I itch to knock 70p off the price tag.

Clearsprings Cape Red NV

Clos Malverne Auret Cabernet Sauvignon/Pinotage 1996

Such richness and aplomb must rate well. The exotic edge to the fruit, the positive, well balanced tannins and the flourish on the finish. Very classy stuff. Only at Wine Cellar stores.

SOUTH AFRICAN RED

Constantia Uitsig Merlot 1996 　16　E

Extremely impressive and for a tenner not absurdly priced. The merlot in this specimen is gently peppery, rich, very complex on the finish, dry, smoky, tannic and very classy. Only at Wine Cellar stores.

Louisvale Cabernet Sauvignon/Merlot 1996 　15　E

Mooiplaas Cabernet Sauvignon 1996 　15.5　E

Oak Village Cabernet Sauvignon 1997 　13　C

The Pinotage Company Bush Vine Pinotage 1998 　16　D

Smells like teenage perfume but the fruit on the taste buds is strict, vegetal, very adult, sensuous and very dry and secure. Stunning glugging, all in all. Only at Wine Cellar stores.

SOUTH AFRICAN WINE WHITE

African Legend Sauvignon Blanc 1998 　13　C

Finishes on spindly legs, a bit.

Arniston Bay Chenin Blanc/Chardonnay 1998 　15.5　C

Extremely forward but not flashy. Has warmth and piles of soft fruit but manages to stay refreshing and engagingly plump without being obscenely Rubenesque. Only at Wine Cellar stores.

Brampton Sauvignon Blanc 1997 　14.5　D

Capells Court Chardonnay 1998

Hint of spicy melon on the finish rounds off a rousing performance from a gorgeously textured and tightly woven specimen of top notch quaffing.

Capells Court Sauvignon Blanc 1998

Lovely rich, rousing finish. Not classic, but a terrific food wine.

Hartenberg 'Occasional' Pinot Blanc 1997

Interesting fruit here: creamy yet crisp. How it achieves this paradox I cannot say but the taste buds revel in it.

L'Avenir Chardonnay 1997

Woody and winsome.

Savanha Barrel Fermented Chardonnay 1998

Bit too chewy and rich for the faint-palated but with Thai food it would be unput-downable. Wine Rack and Bottoms Up only.

Spice Route Long Walk Sauvignon Blanc 1998

Fabulous fruit: juicy and ripe, yet subtle and clinging. Selected stores.

Stowells of Chelsea Chenin Blanc (3-litre box)

Price band is the equivalent for 75cl.

Van Loveren Pinot Gris 1998

SPANISH WINE   RED

Castillo de Liria Valencia NV   `14.5` B

Chivite Navarra Vina Marcos 1997   `13` C

Conde de Valdemar Rioja Crianza 1996   `13.5` D

Too hard for these tender lips. Selected stores.

Fallers Leap Valdepusa Tempranillo 1995   `13` C

Touch of cough mixture as it quits the throat.

Gran Fuedo Reserva 1994   `12` D

**La Tasca, Oak Aged, Vino de la Tierra de
Manchuela 1996**   `11` B

Navajas Rioja Crianza 1995   `15.5` D

Always one of the most charmingly aromatic and smoothly
flavoursome of riojas.

Retuerta Abadia, Rivola 1996   `16` D

Sheer textured class here. Fruit of towering quality and elegant
texture, like silk, it's a great investment for the palate which
pays off immediately. Only at Wine Cellar and Martha's Vineyard stores.

Roble Tempranillo 1996   `15` C

Senorio de Robles Jumilla 1997   `15.5` B

SPANISH WINE WHITE

Campo Viejo Barrel Fermented Viura 1997

What a wonderfully rich yet fresh-edged and ripe wine – polished and dry, rich and full – a great balancing act. Selected stores.

Casa Rural White NV

Superb value for money. Chewy, fresh, impish, delightfully clean and with a hint of exotic pineapple on the finish. Selected stores.

Dominio di Montalvo Rioja, Campo Viejo 1995

Hate that chewy woodiness.

Ed's White 1996

Lagar de Cervera, Albarino Rias Baixas 1996

Rioja Montalvo Limited Edition 1995

Woody and somewhat chewy, this wine calls for food of richness and spiciness.

Siesta Viura, Vino de la Tierra de Manchuela 1996

Vinas del Vero Barrel Fermented Chardonnay, Somontano 1996

Lovely harmony of elements, rich, but with enough zip on the

265

finish to give it a lilting, companionable charm. Wine Cellars and Martha's Vineyard only.

Vinas del Vero Macabeo/Chardonnay, Somontano 1996

USA WINE RED

Blossom Hill Californian Red NV

Eagle Peak Merlot, Fetzer Vineyards 1997

Decidedly chewy yet very soft and warm. Curious paradox of styles: seems composty and ripe then goes dry and tannin-teasing, blackcurrant beneath its feet. Delicious stuff. Selected stores.

Fetzer Home Ranch Zinfandel 1996

Lovely spicy fruit here. Dry yet full of flavour and textured ripeness.

Fetzer Valley Oaks Cabernet Sauvignon 1997

One of the most civilised, less barbarous, cabernets around.

Redwood Trail Pinot Noir 1997

Cherryish and not far from being an interesting pinot.

Talus Zinfandel 1996

Selected stores.

Talus Zinfandel 1997

Very juicy and rampant.

Vendange Californian Red 1998

Very dry and peppery and it will perform well with rich food.

Woodbridge Mondavi Zinfandel 1996

Terrific tannins here.

USA WINE   WHITE

Columbia Crest Chardonnay 1997

Loads of warm, friendly fruit, humming with flavours, texture and a lush lingering strawberry/melonicity.

Fetzer Echo Ridge Sauvignon 1997

Hints of a class act.

Fetzer Sundial Chardonnay, 1998 `16` `D`

Always as full of sun as the face of a California beachbum, this is fruit modelled on richness, warmth, and the flavours of the tropics. This vintage has a lovely freshness to it. Selected stores.

St Supery Sauvignon Blanc 1997 `13` `E`

Too expensive for the style.

Vendanges White Zinfandel 1998 `10` `C`

Selected stores.

FORTIFIED WINE

Dows Crusted 1991 `16` `F`

A gorgeous Christmas present: rich, deep, figgy and not oversweet.

Dows LBV 1992 `13.5` `F`

Grahams Malvedos 1984 `13.5` `G`

Quinta de Vargellas Vintage Port 1986 `15` `G`

Taylors Quinta de Terra Feita 1986 `17` `G`

Like taking a draught of liquidised hedgerow plus sun, an allotment of herbs and even a hint of very soft, beautifully developed tannins. The texture is balsamic and gripping, the effect is heady, the residual memory is of doing something rather naughty.

Warres Traditional LBV 1984 `15` `G`

SPARKLING WINE/CHAMPAGNE

Blossom Hill Sparkling NV (USA) `13` `D`

Touch sweet.

Bollinger Grande Cuvee 1990 `14` `H`

Has a fat, plummy undertone. Forty-two quid? Bit rich.

Bollinger RD 1985 `13` `H`

Too dry and austere. Martha's Vineyard only.

Bollinger Special Cuvee NV `14` `H`

It is fine and dry.

Canard Duchene Charles VII NV `14.5` `H`

Very good. Martha's Vineyard only.

Cava Brut NV `15` `C`

Charles Heidsieck Mis en Caves 1995 `13` `H`

**Cool Ridge Sparkling Chardonnay Pinot
Noir Brut NV (Hungary)** `12` `C`

Not as dry or as elegant as Cavas at the same price.

Cuvee Napa Brut, Mumm NV `16` `E`

So much more assertive, refined, tasty and sanely priced than its French cousin I'm surprised there aren't serious riots in Rheims.

Cuvee Napa Rose, Mumm NV `14` `E`

Deutz Marlborough Cuvee NV `13.5` `F`

Has a faintly fleshy finish.

Gosset Grande Millesime 1989 `15` `H`

Better than Krug – rather taut and fine. Martha's Vineyard only.

Gosset Grande Reserve NV　　　14　H

Rather fine. Available in magnum size also.

Green Point Brut 1996　　　15　F

Expensive as a cheap Champagne – but much better fruit.

Krug Grande Cuvee NV　　　13　H

Decent enough at £20 – no more.

Krug Vintage 1989　　　13.5　H

La Corunna Cava NV　　　15　C

Very alert bubbly of dry elegance and with a faint edge of richness. A bargain.

Lanson Vintage Gold Label 1993　　　13.5　H

Bit light on the finish but very dry and classically tight-lipped.

Louis Roederer Brut Vintage 1993 (magnum)　　　13　H

Very warm and toasty on the finish.

Marquis de la Tour Brut (France)　　　13　C

Marquis de la Tour Demi Sec NC (France)　　　8　C

A touch revolting.

Marquis de la Tour Rose NV (France)　　　14　C

Piper Heidsieck Rare 1985　　　17　H

My favourite: toast, nuts, fruit, finesse, dry, liveliness, not too old – perfect maturity. Martha's Vineyard only.

Pol Roger Sir Winston Churchill Cuvee 1988   `16` `H`

Immensely proud, dry, witty, plump yet fleet of foot. Goes extremely well with cucumber sandwiches with mint. Also smoked salmon. Martha's Vineyard only.

Pol Roger White Foil   `11` `H`

Pommery Vintage 1991   `12` `H`

Not good enough. Too coarse.

Seaview Brut Rose   `14` `D`

Veuve Clicquot La Grande Dame 1990   `16` `H`

Rather lovely – achieves dryness yet texture and a suggestion of fruit.

WINE CELLAR

Nader Haghighi, the chief executive of Parisa, the company which runs Wine Cellar among other off-licence formats, was a frustrated man last October. He had been an extremely vocal opponent of the merger of Thresher and Victoria Wine and was disappointed to say the least when my then, now quondam, neighbour Peter Mandelson, at that time Trade and Industry Secretary, approved the pairing (a marriage now operating under the sobriquet First Quench which when my ten-year-old saw this on a letterhead said, 'Daddy, is that supposed to be a joke?'). Mr Haghighi does not, however, have a sense of humour about this pun. He wrote letters to independent off-licence operators all over the country in an attempt to mobilise action against the merger. In a report in *Off-Licence News* in October 1998, he said of the decision: 'I think it very much shows the way the government operates in these matters. Irrespective of any representations made by trade suppliers and independent operators, they were of the view that it should go ahead.' As an outsider, I can only admit to a certain puzzlement at this sort of reaction to powerful competition. It's like a tennis player complaining about Greg Rusedski's service. You just have to deal with it.

Many people, however, share Mr Haghighi's misgivings about the formation of huge powerful combines and the effect they have on independent retailers. But it has to be said that Mr Haghighi does not come across as someone who has been oppressed by rampant capitalism. He is clearly an ambitious businessman – a fact most clearly illustrated by the strong rumours that he himself was at one stage planning takeover bids for both Thresher and Victoria Wine. Even now he is mooted as a possible future bidder for the entire First Quench group. Is it remotely possible that Parisa has the resources, or could borrow them, to finance such a bid? The fact that rumours like this ignite and are not immediately dampened is surely, in part, fuelled by the burning ambition of the individual or company about whom speculation is most rife. Such speculations also, I guess, excite backers to believe that no stone is being left unturned by the company in its search to maximise its worth, weight, market share, and, ultimately, return to shareholders. One should not forget that Thresher was a company Mr Haghighi himself joined as a part-time assistant in 1981, ending up as its operations director eight years later. If the unlikely did happen and his company ended up owning Thresher it would be irony in the extreme.

At present, however, he is concerning himself with the development of Parisa, the company which was created by the £56 million management buyout, which Mr Haghighi himself led, of the Greenalls Cellars off licence business in August 1997. Parisa operates nearly 500 stores in several different formats. There are 54 Wine Cellar stores and around 130 Booze Buster discount off licences as well as the Cellar 5 off licences, Right Choice convenience stores, Night Vision off licence/video shops and Berkeley Wines drinks stores.

Back in May 1998, *Off-Licence News* reported that Parisa was planning to add at least two new retail formats, a drinks superstore and a cafe/bar concept. Mr Haghighi believes that the off licence sector has not been innovative enough in the face of competition from supermarkets. He said in an interview with *Checkout* magazine in August 1998: 'I think that most off licence chains are nothing more than very basic retailers of alcohol; over the years, they have traded on the similarities between each other. If one chain does something the rest tend to copy. We are not innovative enough as a sector.' Presumably, this censure would exclude Oddbins which has surely been the most organically innovative of wine chains and has seen many of its ideas copied by competitors.

As indeed has Majestic. They have pioneered the wine warehouse concept in the UK and Parisa has noted this. It was first thought that Parisa's 5,000 sq ft superstores would be called Super Booze Buster after the company's existing discount drinks stores but the company later said the new format would trade under the name Mega Drinks Warehouse. The company had originally said that the first superstore would be open by the end of summer 1998 but in the autumn there was still no sign of one though Parisa reaffirmed its commitment to the idea in an article in *Off-Licence News* in October 1998.

However, by February 1999 the company appeared to have put its superstore plans on hold as it concentrated on developing the cafe/bar format. Parisa had already broken new ground for UK wine shops when it introduced cafe/bar sections in its Wine Cellar stores. The idea is that by paying a modest corkage charge, customers can buy any wine for consumption on the premises. In February 1999, 15 of the 54 Wine Cellar outlets had licensed cafe areas. Now Parisa has taken this a stage further with the launch of the Parisa Cafe Bar. The Parisa bar concept combines the cafe/bar environment with take-home sales and also includes an in-store micro-brewery. The first such store opened in Putney in October 1998 and in February the company said that it had been encouraged by its performance.

Although Parisa told *Off-Licence News* in February that there was fierce competition for sites suitable for the Parisa bar concept, it clearly was not going to let this stand in its way. In June, the group announced that it planned to open Parisa Cafe Bars in five locations creating 200 jobs. Cafes were scheduled to open in Newbury, Bromley, Wilmslow, Harpenden and Leeds before the end of July. Leeds certainly opened because I was invited, along with many other food and wine writers I imagine, to the 'celebrity' opening of this branch. I was unable to attend due to family commitments and I admit to feeling somewhat inept that I have yet to visit a single one of Parisa's wine bars, even though I have cycled past the Putney one several times. The main idea behind the concept is that it offers a wide range of wines at well below the normal prices charged in the on-trade. 'We sell wine in our Parisa Cafe Bars at prices comparable to those charged in our off licences,' Mr Haghighi says. 'The only difference is a standard £3 corkage charge on each bottle. We think this gives us a competitive advantage that will strike a chord with our customers.' The company also said the Parisa Cafe Bars offer an extensive menu of chef-prepared dishes and operate a strict ban on the sale of genetically modified foods.

In May, Parisa announced that it was increasing its selection of vegetarian and vegan wines. The company said it wanted vegetarians and vegans to have a wider choice and more information about the wines before they buy. Staff at the company's Wine Cellar and Berkeley Wines stores are being informed which wines are suitable for vegetarians and for vegans. Good news.

I applaud all these moves and I certainly stand four-square behind any food business which wants to lower the cost of restaurant wine drinking. It is scandalous that restaurants can routinely charge three times the shop price for wine before any service charge is chucked in. In one preposterous example of overcharging, in an extreme eatery in west London, I noted that the wine list asked £250 for a magnum of Chilean wine which costs £10 the bottle in a supermarket. If Parisa can operate wine bars where good food is the norm and customers can get away with a reasonable corkage charge on a good range of wines bought next door, then I am all for it. I would certainly relish the idea of trogging across to Putney to pay £9.99 (excluding corkage) for a bottle of Wine Cellar's Leasingham Estate Cabernet/Malbec along with a dish of roasted vegetables with melted cheese, garlic and herbs. The trick now is to have several hundred of these Wine Bars up and running, no uniform menus or fascias but local and regional differences and ethnic diversity, with a range of terrific wines where customers don't mind paying £8 or £9 for wine they can't get in a supermarket. This last part is essential for the success of such a venture.

I do, however, question some of the things Mr Haghighi was reported as saying in an interview he gave in Spring to the magazine *Harpers on Retail*. Talking of low retail wine prices (one eye on the supermarkets I assume) he said: 'Using buying power to cut margins with the aim of increasing volume in the short term is putting the squeeze on suppliers to do the same. This means that suppliers will lack sufficient funds to invest in technology and innovating their product categories and consumers will be faced with the same products year on year. We've already witnessed this in the market place for the past few years where product development has been seriously limited.'

I would aver that the evidence contradicts this. Firstly, buying power is not a short term expedient. It is a long-term strategic weapon to increase customer loyalty and repeat purchase and also to firmly cement buyer/supplier relations. Second, suppliers are not hampered in their investment potential, on the contrary. For example, when I visited Bulgaria – a country which has been supplying cheap wine to the UK for thirty years – just before this introduction went to the printer I saw new ideas abounding, old wineries ready for refurbishment, and even the building of a vast new winery of utter state-of-the-art technology. It is buying power, millions of bottles of wine, payment on time on a single invoice by a massive UK supplier, which provides the confidence for banks to supply the capital for this kind of investment. Far from we drinkers being faced with the same old wines year on year, we face an abundance, a plethora even, of new products. Product development has not been limited. It has been burgeoning like never before. Wine departments in most UK wine retailers have been busy developing new wines and, in many cases, exclusive new brands of wine which will seriously challenge, over the coming years, the established wine brands like Gallo and Piat d'Or.

When Mr Haghighi is reported as saying in the same interview: 'Suppliers need to consider how they can support the small players to help them survive' he is right and one way is to develop brands exclusive to your wine bars and wine shops. This has already been achieved with Parisa's micro-brewed Parisa Ales range as well as the Wine Cellar Bin 1 Riesling and Bin 2 Shiraz from the Miranda winery in Australia. I agree 'small players' should not go to the wall, but this only applies to efficient, market-empathetic players. To judge from his idea of wine bar eateries, Mr Haghighi is one such but couldn't the own-label Wine Cellar range be greatly expanded?

Of all the retailers I cover, this one is the most shrouded in mystery and uncertainty. I have never had a letter from any reader about them (putting Parisa in a unique category). Mr David Vaughan, who buys the wine, is a competent individual of experience and skill but he does not seem to get the chance to spread his wings as widely as that experience clearly warrants. The wine list is a design mess, with poorly photographed sponsored recipes too dominant. There are few own-labels here as I have already said and the price points are higher than competitors (the average per-bottle price being £5.99, much greater than supermarkets and also above Majestic's which is just over a fiver). In the end, I can only rate a wine retailer by its wines and the ratings of the wines which follow say everything I can about this one.

Wine Cellar (Parisa Limited)
PO Box 476
Loushers Lane
Warrington
Cheshire WA4 6RQ
Tel: 01925 444555
Fax: 01925 415 474
e-mail: gf95@dial.pipex.com

ARGENTINIAN WINE RED

Etchart Cafayate Cabernet Sauvignon 1995 `14` `D`

Savoury and thickly carpeted under tongue.

Etchart Rio de Plata Malbec 1996 `13` `C`

Finishes a touch ho-humly.

Rutini Merlot 1995 `13.5` `D`

A lot of loot for such straightforwardly pleasing £4.99 fruit. Has some nice tannins, though.

Valentin Bianchi Cabernet Sauvignon 1996 `16` `E`

Very posh, potent and beautifully polished. Speaks with a very elegant plum in its mouth.

ARGENTINIAN WINE WHITE

Rutini Chardonnay 1997 `13.5` `D`

Very florid and plump. Needs food.

AUSTRALIAN WINE RED

Bethany Vineyards Shiraz 1996 `13.5` `F`

A lot of money for a six quid wine – at which price this soft, aromatic, gently spicy wine would rate 15 at least.

Penfolds Bin 35 Cabernet Sauvignon/ Shiraz/Ruby Cabernet 1997 `14` `D`

Juicy and well-meaning.

Peter Lehmann Vine Vale Grenache 1998 `15.5` `C`

Hint of leather, spice and rich, very rich, damson fruit. Jam of a highly sophisticated kind.

Rosemount Estate Grenache/Shiraz 1998 `15` `D`

Yes, it's immensely juicy but fine tannins interrupt the flood – well in time.

Rothbury Hunter Valley Shiraz 1996 `13` `E`

Very juicy and soft. Needs food. But what? Curried emu?

Wolf Blass Green Label Shiraz 1996 `14` `D`

A juicy wine for curries – little else.

AUSTRALIAN WINE WHITE

Capel Vale Verdelho 1998 `16.5` `E`

This is a lovely, softly textured, gently spicy artefact of immense charm.

Hardys Padthaway Chardonnay 1997   `15.5` `E`

Hints of wood and dry lemon overcoating with rich and elegant fruit.

Hardys Stamp of Australia Chardonnay Semillon 1998   `15.5` `C`

Delicious! Unusually complex yet modern and fresh. Has layers of melon (not overripe) and what seems like a hint of raspberry. Good acidity buffers this fruity attack.

Nanya Estate Colombard/Chardonnay 1997   `10` `B`

Morbleu! Zis ees vin?

CHILEAN WINE RED

Mapocho Cabernet Sauvignon 1997   `14` `C`

Marvellous spicy food wine, in spite of its dry fruit, crude perfume and roustabout manners. It's the finish which makes it food-friendly.

Mapocho Merlot 1997   `13` `C`

Odd smell (seems to be a Mapocho trait) and the fruit falls over itself. But with food it might be fine.

Montgras Reserve Cabernet Sauvignon 1997   `15` `D`

Juicy, yet savoury and tannic, textured and tightly tailored. Has loads of warm, soft fruit with a hint of worldliness.

Santa Ines Legado de Armida Cabernet Sauvignon Reserve 1997　16.5　D

Surely one of the most impressive reds at this retailer. It has that insouciant Chilean way of mixing weight with wit, texture with tension, fruit with serious layers of meaning.

FRENCH WINE　　　　　　RED

Anjou Cabernet Franc Les Trois Saisons 1997　14.5　C

Lovely bitter cherry and raspberry-edged richness. A real characterful glugging wine (and good with food).

Big Frank's Cabernet Franc 1997　16　D

Delicious tobacco and heather-fruited specimen. Has finesse yet evident character and richness. Most impressive texturally.

Calvet Reserve Rouge 1996　13　D

Touch dull and flat on the finish.

Chasse du Pape Cotes du Rhone, Meffre 1997　12　C

Weak vintage of what has been a terrific red. The tannins in this manifestation have overtaken the juicy fruit.

Chateau Cotes de Bellevue, Cotes de Bourg 1996　13.5　D

Overpriced by two pounds at least for the level of fruit on offer.

Chateau Lamargue Costieres de Nimes 1997   15   C

Juicy yet tightly and firmly controlled by ripe subtle tannins and good acidity. A very agreeable structured quaffer.

Domaine de Bacarra Beaujolais Villages 1997   11   D

Tries hard – at six quid it's a bit loose.

Fleurie Domaine de la Bouroniere 1998   11   E

Shocking price for fruit of this vulgarity.

Hautes Cotes de Nuits, Y. Chalet 1996   12   E

Simplistic fruit at nigh on nine quid.

La Ciboise Rouge, Chapoutier 1997   15   C

Curiously delicious raspberry-rich finish to some elegant fruit.

Port Neuf Rouge   13   B

Rhone Valley Red VdP de Vaucluse NV   13   C

A party wine at a non-party price (alas). Has some drinkable qualities.

Thierry & Guy Utter Bastard Syrah 1998   14.5   D

Very polished in the mouth, though the finish is all of a piece and doesn't startle or develop new strands of flavour.

Wild Pig Barrel Reserve Syrah 1997   16   C

Beautifully smooth and relaxed. Nary a hint of earth nor even of tannin. A most polished performer of texture and style.

FRENCH WINE   WHITE

Calvet Reserve Blanc 1998   12 C

Pretty dull.

Domaine de Tariquet Sauvignon 1998   14 C

Pert and polished – with solid sauvignon freshness.

**Domaine l'Orgeril Reserve Chardonnay,
VdP d'Oc 1997**   12 D

Goes a bit squashy and bruised on the finish.

**Honore de Berticot Semillon, Cotes de
Duras 1998**   14 C

Unusually chewy fruit makes the texture of this wine good for
all sorts of dishes from salads to grilled prawns.

**Orchid Vale Medium Dry Chardonnay
1998**   13 C

Bit adolescent and sweetly-intentioned for me.

Port Neuf White   14.5 B

Rhone Valley White, VdP de Vaucluse NV   11 C

Very cosmetic and tarty.

GREEK WINE RED

Hatzimichalis Cabernet Sauvignon 1997

Most individual: rich, dry, herby, warm, complex, multi-layered and full of savoury surprises. An elegant, authoritative cabernet.

Sillogi Lafazanis Red 1997

Dry and reaches for fruit rather than whole-heartedly grabbing it.

St George Skouras, Nemea 1996

Excellent perfume, mid-palate fruit, and rousing tannins in the back of the throat. Good red for those spicy Greek sausages.

GREEK WINE WHITE

Hatzimichalis Chardonnay 1998

Absurd price for such sticky fruit.

Sillogi Lafazanis White 1998

Rather muddled and uncertain.

285

HUNGARIAN WINE RED

Chapel Hill Cabernet Sauvignon 1996 9 C

Getting old and raisiny. Shouldn't be on sale.

HUNGARIAN WINE WHITE

Chapel Hill Irsai Oliver 1997 14.5 B

Clean, fresh. crisp, floral-edged – a lovely simple aperitif glug.

Chapel Hill Sauvignon Blanc 1997 13 C

ITALIAN WINE RED

D'Istinto Sangiovese/Merlot 1997 (Sicily) 15.5 C

**Duca di Castelmonte Cent'are Rosso
1996 (Sicily)** 15 C

ITALIAN WINE WHITE

Monte Tenda Soave 1998 12 C

Falls a bit flat on the finish.

Puglian Bianco Cantele, Kim Milne

NEW ZEALAND WINE WHITE

Delegat's Reserve Chardonnay 1997

Lot of loot for a sour-puss chardonnay – but it is good with food.

Montana Reserve Chardonnay 1997

Very chewy and woody and the planks show through the soft fruit carpet here and there, but with fish on the plate it would be fine.

Oyster Bay Sauvignon Blanc 1998

Quite lively richness yet restrained fluency of rippling fruit.

PORTUGUESE WINE RED

Alianca Palmela Paticular 1992

Portada Tinto Estremadura 1995

Great value here. An aromatic, gorgeously soft, rich, ripe wine with a walloping fruity finish.

Quinta do Vale da Raposa 1995

SOUTH AFRICAN WINE   RED

Clos Malverne Cabernet/Shiraz 1997   14.5   D

Spicy, rich, hedgerow-fruity and thick, this is a good wine for
elegant Indian dishes.

First River Winery Stellenbosch Dry Red   14   C

Klein Gustrow Cabernet/Merlot 1994   15   E

Very rich and dry, good tannins, and the fruit thwacks the back
of the throat in ripe yet layered style.

L'Avenir Cabernet Sauvignon 1996   13   E

Juicy and ripe, it seems expensive at eight quid.

Paradyskloof Cabernet Sauvignon/Merlot
1997   13.5   D

Juice with a hint of attitude. Suits roast chicken stuffed with
kumquats.

SOUTH AFRICAN WINE   WHITE

Constantia Reserve Chardonnay 1996   10   E

Bit muddy and moody on the finish.

Fairview Colombard 1998   14   C

Oddly fat for Fairview. Needs food.

Neil Ellis Sauvignon Blanc 1998

Touches of nicely mown grass to the finish. A good wine for shellfish.

SPANISH WINE RED

De Muller Cabernet Sauvignon Tarragona 1996

Very brisk and tannic, with subsumed subtleties cowed by the outward elements rather than boosted by the inner.

Montalvo Reserva Rioja 1994

Good chewiness of the tannins and some elegant vanilla stitching to the well-tailored fruit.

Ondarre Reserva Rioja 1994

Expensive and juicy.

Ondarre 'Rivallana' Crianza Rioja 1996

Very creamy juice with a hint of yoghurt and vanilla.

SPANISH WINE WHITE

De Muller Chardonnay 1997

Big, chewy food wine – great with tandoori prawns.

SWISS WINE   RED

Pinot Noir Trilogy 1996   `12` `D`

USA WINE   RED

Clos du Val Le Clos NV   `14` `E`

Fetzer Pinot Noir, Santa Barbara 1996   `13` `D`

**Fetzer Valley Oaks Cabernet Sauvignon
1996**   `16.5` `D`

Warm, all-embracing, deep, broad, and most charmingly well-
textured and ripe on the finish.

**Fetzer Valley Oaks Cabernet Sauvignon
1996**   `16.5` `D`

Warm, all-embracing, deep, broad, and most charmingly well-
textured and ripe on the finish. Superstores only.

**Gallo Sonoma Barrelli Creek Cabernet
Sauvignon 1994**   `15.5` `F`

A most sveltely textured, finely wrought specimen at the peak
of maturity. An expensive treat for the Christmas fowl, it has
sturdiness, complexity, weight (yet finesse) and lovely warm
tannins.

Gallo Sonoma County Pinot Noir 1995   `13.5` `E`

Better than many Nuits-St-Georges but that's not saying a lot.
It has some bite and an echo of feral fruit on the finish.

Gallo Sonoma Frei Ranch Cabernet Sauvignon 1994

14 F

Highly drinkable and mature, if expensive. It has raisins and blackcurrants, good brisk tannins, and some wit to its finish.

Paul Thomas Cabernet/Merlot 1995

14 E

Willamette Pinot Noir 1995

15.5 E

USA WINE
WHITE

Chateau St Michelle Chardonnay 1995

15 D

Gallo Sonoma County Chardonnay 1995

10 E

Lost its freshness – gone to fat and frowstiness.

Quady Essensia Orange Muscat, California 1996 (half bottle)

16 D

Excellent keeping qualities with its waxy, candied orange peel fruit and rich acidity – say ten years or so – but great now with fresh fruit – or a creme brulee.

Quady Starboard Batch 88, California (half bottle)

15 C

STOP PRESS

FULLERS

AUSTRALIAN WINE WHITE

Rosemount Chardonnay 1998   `16` `D`

Utterly scrumptious fruit. Improved a bit since I tasted it last spring, too.

CHILEAN WINE RED

Casa Lapostolle Cabernet Sauvignon 1997   `17` `D`

Wonderful texture. Very exciting experience.

Casa Lapostolle Cuvee Alexandre Cabernet Sauvignon 1997   `16.5` `E`

Superb chewy fruit.

Casa Lapostolle Merlot 1998   `16.5` `D`

Gorgeous tannins.

CHILEAN WINE   WHITE

Casa Lapostolle Chardonnay 1998   `18.5` `D`

Sheer magic!

**Casa Lapostolle Cuvee Alexandre
Chardonnay 1997**   `17.5` `E`

One of Chile's greatest chardonnays. Has superb balance (richness, ripeness, length of flavour) and it's so classy it hurts.

Casa Lapostolle Sauvignon Blanc 1999   `17` `D`

Even more complex than the '98, more svelte.

ITALIAN WINE   WHITE

Mezzo Mondo Chardonnay 1998   `15.5` `C`

Gorgeous freshness with a hint of fat melon and waxy lemon. Improving nicely in bottle (qv the main section of this book).

MAJESTIC

FRENCH WINE RED

Bois de Lamothe Cabernet Franc, Cotes de Duras 1998

Stunning bargain: subtly spiced, cherry fruit of class and fair concentration. Gluggable, food-friendly, deep and rich, yet lithe and unpretentious.

Chateau Haut La Graviere Haut-Medoc 1995

More acidity and liveliness than its Bourg brother and it has almost a sweet disposition in comparison. The fruit is very soft and ripe and most deliciously untypical.

Chateau La Graviere Cotes de Bourg 1995

At the peak of its charms – the tannins have softened and will wilt within a year. The fruit is dry, not remotely austere or difficult. A glugging claret.

Chateau Laporte St Emilion 1995

Mature, ripe, assertive yet fully integrated tannins, fruit and acidity of surprising texture and richness. Cherries/plums/herbs, hint of earth, touch of smoke. An excellent claret for the money.

FRENCH WINE WHITE

Bois de Lamothe Sauvignon Blanc, VdP du Lot et Garonne 1997

Intense gooseberry perfume and delicious rich fruit. A real party-with-canapes wine. Exuberant company for anything from Thai chicken on a stick to grilled prawns.

Cotes du Rhone Rosé Guigal 1997

Classy texture and rich fruit – great with Thai food or fish dishes. It's got a dry, thick, cherry jam edge.

ITALIAN WINE RED

Bragnolo Azienda San Biagio 1997

Tired of cabs and merls? Try this sangiovese plus blend. It'll knock your socks off.

Chianti Il Tasso 1998

A very juicy richness here with only echoes of the baked earth typicity of the breed.

Chianti Rufina Basciano 1997

Delayed action richness from a complex wine of vigour and dash. The texture, the tannins are excellent.

Conero Conti Cortesi 1997

Savoury, jammy, very ripe – but but but . . . those glorious tannins buttress the building beautifully.

Dolcetto d'Alba de Forville 1998

The spiky tannins stud the rich fruit like spicy currants in a chocolate cake.

Merlot del Veneto Marchesini 1998

Very juicy and charming.

Primitivo del Salento Sigillo Primo 1998

Big, rich, rousing, soft, cockle-warming (yet young and fresh), cheeky and utterly drinkable.

Sassaiolo Rosso Piceno 1997

A wonderfully jammy spicy food wine.

Teroldego Rotaliano La Bottega de'Vinai 1998

More Italian juice. '98 must be the year for it.

Valpolicella Superiore Classico Bussola 1996

Ten quid for the best straight valpol you'll ever dip your beak into? So it is. The ripeness and the sheer satin texture make it a marvellous food wine.

ITALIAN WINE   WHITE

Ca'Visco Soave Classico Superiore Coffele 1998

Intense concentration of texture and rich, serious fruit. Very elegant, very striking.

Chardonnay di Puglia, Pasqua 1998

A wine as bright and on the button as the vivid label.

Frascati Superiore, Selciatella 1998

Superior indeed: lush, ripe fruit with superb crisp acids. Dry yet fruity.

Piemonte Chardonnay de Forville 1998

Very chewy and individual. Not big or bouncy but delicate and nervously strung together (fruit and acid).

Pinot Grigio Alois Lageder 1998

Astonishing level of nutty, peachy fruit. Beautifully supple and textured.

PORTUGUESE WINE RED

Contes de Cima Vinho Regional Alentejano 1997

Cinnamon-coated, rich fruit of quite lush and forward intentions. Needs spicy food.

SPANISH WINE RED

Dardell Syrah Cabernet Grenache Terra Alta 1998

Outguns many an Aussie shiraz with its wonderful balsamic texture, gripping fruit, smooth tannins and explosive finish.

'G' Dehesa Gago Telmo Rodriguez 1998

The bullish wit of the label does nothing to prepare you for the surprise of the earthy riches in the bottle. Rustic? Only a touch. Finely knitted yet powerful.

Ochoa Tempranillo Garnache Navarra 1998

Hints of roasted nut on the finish which completes a medley of mature, richer gifts.

Onix Priorato Vinicola del Priorat 1998

A juicy style, smooth and not clodhopping or too alcoholic (which priorats can be). Too refined? Perhaps. But it's a wonderful robust wine for robust people.

Vina El Salado Extremadura 1998

Takes a few seconds for the fruit to enrich the throat, but the wait is worthwhile. Hugely lap-uppable fruit.

ODDBINS

AUSTRALIAN WINE RED

Preece Cabernet Sauvignon 1996 `14` `E`

Wirra Wirra Church Block Cabernet Shiraz Merlot 1997 `16.5` `E`

A wonderful blend of striking richness and very stylish tannins. Aromatic, all-action and endearing (but not *too* dear). Improving nicely in bottle, too (qv the main section of this book).

Wolf Blass Shiraz 1996 `14` `D`

CHILEAN WINE RED

Casa Lapostolle Cabernet Sauvignon 1997 `17` `D`

Wonderful texture. Very exciting experience.

Casa Lapostolle Cuvee Alexandre Cabernet Sauvignon 1997 `16.5` `E`

Superb chewy fruit.

Casa Lapostolle Cuvee Alexandre Merlot 1997 `17.5` `F`

The sheer naked hedonistic level of polish on this wine's leather is simply world class. Won't age much – so drink it before 2000 – with friends and fowls.

Casa Lapostolle Merlot 1998 16.5 D

Gorgeous tannins.

CHILEAN WINE WHITE

Casa Lapostolle Chardonnay 1998 18.5 D

Sheer magic!

Casa Lapostolle Cuvee Alexandre Chardonnay 1997 17.5 E

One of Chile's greatest chardonnays. Has superb balance (richness, ripeness, length of flavour) and it's so classy it hurts. Has improved in bottle, too, since I first tasted it (qv the main section of this book).

Casa Lapostolle Sauvignon Blanc 1999 17 D

Even more complex than the '98, more svelte.

GREEK WINE WHITE

Thalassitis Santorini Assyrtiko 1998 15.5 D

Deliciously different. The firm fruit spreads on the finish, turns chewy and lemony and gently rich, yet undertoning it all is a mineral pool of finesse and fluidity. A class act.

PORTUGUESE WINE RED

Terra Franca NV

Tame on first opening, it needs a couple of hours to get into some rich, dry, tobacco-edged richness and textured charm.

SOUTH AFRICAN WINE RED

Kumala Reserve Cabernet Sauvignon 1998

Curious ambivalence here: youthful exuberance with seasoned mellowness. The wine offers ripe plum, subtle tobacco nuances, hint of chocolate and tea (lapsang souchong) and a smoothness of almost smug hauteur. For all that, nine quid is a lot of money. It can be opened and decanted five to six hours beforehand.

SPARKLING WINE/CHAMPAGNE

Yellowglen Vintage Brut 1995 (Australia)

Big, rich, mouthfilling, almost rampantly plump fruit. Hardly classic but with food it might be a triumph. Even jellied eels, though, will be swamped by the wine's energy.

THRESHER

CHILEAN WINE   RED

**Casa Lapostolle Cuvee Alexandre
Cabernet Sauvignon 1997**   `16.5` `E`

Superb chewy fruit.

**Casa Lapostolle Cuvee Alexandre
Merlot 1997**   `17.5` `F`

The sheer naked hedonistic level of polish on this wine's leather
is simply world class. Won't age much – so drink it before 2000
– with friends and fowls.

Casa Lapostolle Merlot 1998   `16.5` `D`

Gorgeous tannins.

Cono Sur Cabernet Sauvignon, Rapel 1998 `16.5` `C`

Terrific tannins, evolved and vibrant, combined with cassis and
tobacco fruitiness. It's improved in bottle, too, since the summer
(cf the main section of this book).

CHILEAN WINE WHITE

Casa Lapostolle Sauvignon Blanc 1999

Even more complex than the '98, more svelte.

NEW ZEALAND WINE WHITE

Montana Reserve Chardonnay 1998

Exceptional style of fruit where the depth remains dry, retains complexity, finishes with rich promise. Much improved since I tasted it last summer (cf the main section of this book).

UNWINS

Vinas del Vero Chardonnay 1998

Sheer charm and coolness here, lovely restrained richness and
balance. Very classy. Has come on tremendously in bottle since
I tasted it last spring (qv the main section of this book).

VICTORIA WINE

AUSTRALIAN WINE   WHITE

Wolf Blass Riesling 1998   `15.5` `D`

A wonderfully richly textured, gently lemony food wine. Still young (two years to peak), it has a fading finish which time will repair. Not at all stores.

CHILEAN WINE   RED

Casa Lapostolle Cuvee Alexandre Cabernet Sauvignon 1997   `16.5` `E`

Superb chewy fruit.

Casa Lapostolle Cuvee Alexandre Merlot 1997   `17.5` `F`

The sheer naked hedonistic level of polish on this wine's leather is simply world class. Won't age much – so drink it before 2000 – with friends and fowls.

Casa Lapostolle Merlot 1998   `16.5` `D`

Gorgeous tannins.

Cono Sur Cabernet Sauvignon, Rapel 1998 C

Terrific tannins, evolved and vibrant, combined with cassis and
tobacco fruitiness. It's improved in bottle, too, since the summer
(qv the main section of this book).

CHILEAN WINE WHITE

Casa Lapostolle Sauvignon Blanc 1999

Even more complex than the '98, more svelte.

NEW ZEALAND WINE WHITE

Montana Reserve Chardonnay 1998 16.5 E

Exceptional style of fruit where the depth remains dry, retains
complexity, finishes with rich promise. Much improved since I
tasted it last summer (qv the main section of this book).
